D1083155

The
TRUTH
about
SCANDAL

The
TRUTH
about
SCANDAL

The Everyday Guide *to* Navigating Business Crises

MELISSA DELAY

ISBN: 978-1-63489-151-6
Library of Congress Catalog Number: 2018952097
Printed in the United States of America
First Printing: 2018
22 21 20 19 18   5 4 3 2 1

Book design by Athena Currier

Wise Ink Creative Publishing.
807 Broadway Street NE, Suite 46
Minneapolis, MN 55413
wiseinkpub.com

To order, visit www.itascabooks.com
or call 1-800-901-3480. Reseller discounts available.

Contents

Introduction

CEO Bill Smith walked into the boardroom with a dreadful look on his face. Judging from the bags under his eyes, he hadn't slept all night.

Just before close of business the day before, Bill had called me in a panic. We had never met before, but he'd heard about me from another CEO. Over the phone, he'd told me that an HR intern had discovered an anonymous employee blog that had gone viral. Most of the posts slammed him for his leadership style. One in particular read, "Bill Smith is a joke. All he does is collect millions while we slave away." A local blogger had alerted the media, and Bill had two voicemails from reporters asking for a comment. Bill wanted to bring his whole team together to debrief and create a plan of action, but I had asked for a private meeting first.

As I sat there, I realized our meeting could go one of two ways. Either Bill would listen to my advice, or he would fire me within fifteen minutes. Now that I was behind the curtain, I fully expected to see him suffering from one of the two personality defects that most CEOs I've met have: an enlarged ego and emotional dissonance.

Bill took the seat directly across from me. He said, "First of all, let me say that nothing is more important to me than this company. I have no idea how this happened, but I plan to find out who started this nasty blog. I don't know who they think they are, messing with me like this. It's ridiculous! People run around here like they've got nothing better to do than attack my character. I won't have it!"

Poor Bill. He seemed to suffer from both defects.

I knew I had to defuse the situation before we could get anywhere, so I started into the same speech I'd given to countless leaders in the past. "I know what you mean, Bill. It isn't right. Employees should be focused on work, not blogging. But there are two truths about employees—and when you know these two truths, most of your difficulties with them will go away. Before I tell you these truths, let me offer you a get-out-of-jail-free card. You see, very few leaders know anything about these truths. Like you, they're busy running a business. And until now, because you haven't had the benefit of this kind of coaching, you have quite possibly been the victim of wrong impressions."

I said all of this to soothe his ego, and it looked like it was working. His shoulders relaxed, and he leaned in, waiting to hear what I would say next.

Now I needed to neutralize his emotions—otherwise he'd never be able to do the hard work of identifying how he had contributed to the situation. Instead, he would just continue blaming the employee who'd started the blog.

Not that I was judging him; we're all this guy. Anytime our identity is threatened, we go into preservation mode. It's just too hard to look inward. It's easier to blame someone else than to do what's right.

So I set about curing his emotional dissonance. I said, "I know you have good intentions, that you mean to connect with your people, and that these posts have little to do with who you really are. It's actually a common occurrence for leaders like you to be attacked for no good reason. But once you know these two truths—the two things that make employees tick—we can go about the process of undoing what's been done."

Finally, it was time to unveil what I was sure he'd never really heard before. "First, employees only want to work for a company they believe cares about them as a person. If they believe that you care about them, they will work hard. If not, they'll be on Craigslist, scanning job boards, goofing off, and ignoring your calls and emails. Second, employees need to see that the work they're doing matters. It has to be about more than punching a clock for eight hours a day. If you make it clear how employees can impact the overall goals of the company, they will work more. It's that simple. That's what makes employees tick. They want to know that you care and that what they do matters."

I summed up my sermon with, "If you keep these truths in mind as you talk with employees, you'll eliminate the risk of having to deal with unsanctioned blog posts."

He puffed up his posture and blurted out, "Well, I knew that."

Great, I thought, *his ego's back.*

This was the moment I was most at risk of getting fired. Leaders like him couldn't help asking themselves,

"*What can she do to help us? I want to know how to get this blog erased from existence, and she's spouting off about whiny employees and their need to be coddled.*"

So I started to ask him questions. "How often do you talk to employees, and what do you say?"

"What do you mean?" he asked. "I talk to employees all the time. I'm constantly telling them 'good job' and thanking them for their work. I guess I don't do it as much as I should, but I'm in back-to-back meetings every day. I don't have a choice. I have thousands of employees. There's no way I can get in front of all of them, so we do this monthly all-employee email."

"And who writes that?" I asked.

"Well, we all do," he said. "My assistant puts it together. She collects all kind of updates from my senior leadership team, and whenever I can, I write a few lines for her to include."

"How well are these emails received?"

He gave the same answer all leaders give. He said, "Everybody loves them."

"Really," I asked. "How do you know?"

"Because they tell me all the time," he replied.

Here we go again, I thought. *Another executive who's certain his communication strategy is right on because his people tell him so.* I needed to burst his bubble— and fast. His leadership team was due to walk through the door any minute. So I began with, "Bless your heart. I can assure you that your all-employee email and other communication efforts are *not* being well received. I know this because of all the nasty comments populating the employee blog you called me in here to address."

The grim look on his face told me he agreed, at least in part, and that we might be making progress. But before I could start laying out the plan, he stopped me. "Wait, there's more. We need to fire our president." Turns out the president had been underperforming for years, but his longtime friendship with the family founders had protected him even after the company went public. However, one month prior, the last remaining family member had retired, and Bill was finally able to move him out of the company without repercussions.

If that wasn't bad enough, Bill's son, the executive vice president of sales, had just been arrested for drunk driving while on a company trip, and his HR director had been advising him for a week to respond with "no comment" to anyone who inquired.

One of the biggest threats to effectively communicating during a scandal is other people. That's because most people have an opinion about how to communicate and believe that, just because they've been speaking since they were two years old, they're an expert. Unfortunately, they're not. To help this guy, I had to get his communication house in order before his team arrived and derailed our efforts.

No one had the power to define Bill except Bill. Employees were trying to do so with the blog, the media would try once they caught wind of the story, and his team would definitely want input. But he couldn't let other people influence what he was going to say—because it wouldn't be authentic and because it would be harder for him to defend.

He needed to decide what he wanted to say. I would refine the message and coach him on to how to stick to it so that it wouldn't matter how badly he was bamboozled. But there wasn't much time. If we had been working together before this incident, we would already have documented his philosophy and core beliefs and would have strong, compelling statements to draw from. But we'd just met.

If I let him, he would tell me that these things already existed for the company. He'd probably even point to a plaque on the wall where they'd been laminated. However, I knew, based on the twenty-minute conversation we'd already had, that they'd be laden with jargon and virtually useless to us.

What we needed to do, and fast, was create some talking points in plain English that would preserve his reputation, defuse the situation, and address the issues he was facing: the employee blog, terminating the president, and his son's drunk driving charge.

I looked at Bill. I could see his furrowed brow and sweaty palms, and I said a series of things that terrified him and relieved him at the same time. "Look, Bill. You need help, and we don't have a lot of time. Your reputation depends upon your ability to deliver the right message at the right time to the right audience."

Bill looked skeptical, but I kept going. "You need messaging to handle each of these conflicts. We're going to craft the basic ones you'll need in the next fifteen minutes. When your team arrives, we'll go into crisis planning mode. I need you to be as transparent as possible. I understand this is difficult, but it's the only way to maintain control of the conversation and get the results you want."

Once he agreed, we set about outlining each of the following:

- A message on the employee blog that spoke directly to readers

- A statement for the press about the blog and his son

- Talking points for his discussion with the president

- A plan to communicate elements of all these issues to his employee base

I told Bill that in order for his messaging to be effective; engage his employees and make them speak favorably about him; avoid negative press or legal actions by the president; and increase productivity rates among all employees, we needed to craft messages that would:

- Tell the truth

- Be considerate

- Use objectivity

Every word Bill spoke or wrote also needed to cast everyone in as favorable a light as possible. If someone else was to blame, Bill needed to be careful about *how* he told the truth, but he still needed to tell the truth. Being as transparent as possible, even about the things you cannot say, is always the right approach.

To keep his reputation intact, Bill couldn't indicate that someone else was to blame. He wouldn't look innocent if he pointed the finger at another person. In our society, we love the underdog—the one who can't defend themselves, who isn't present in the conversation, or who's being picked on. So if Bill pointed the finger at the president or another culprit, he'd inadvertently give them underdog status, helping their cause and hurting his. That's why Bill's messages needed to be considerate of everyone involved. The truth without regard for others is just as bad as a lie.

There are two sides to every story—his side and the blogger's side, his side and the president's side, his son's side and the officer's side—so all his messages needed to state or imply objectivity. By weighing both sides equally, no one would be slighted, emotions would neutralize, and everyone would be able to think clearer. So, without passing any blame, we articulated what was true and good for Bill in the situation and what was true and good for everyone else involved.

The bad news: conflict happens. The good news: about 80 percent of the issues and objections that people can throw at you in any given business crisis can be foreseen. That's what my experience with many companies, including 3M and Carlson, has taught me: 80 percent of crises result from downsizings, product and service mishaps, and all the "what ifs" that we constantly fear but rarely plan for.

In the middle of a business crisis, no one wants to be caught without some valid talking points. As a leader, you need to develop and practice your worst-case scenario responses now so that you will know what to say— at least 80 percent of the time! And you won't have to reinvent the wheel if the situation resurfaces or something similar occurs in the future. All you'll have to do is modify the existing language.

If things are going well for you, take advantage of the moment by thinking ahead. Use this crisis-free time to craft and rehearse the right messages for every imaginable bad-news situation—before you need them. And then, if you ever find yourself in Bill's predicament, follow these steps:

- Gather your team to assess the situation ASAP; include legal counsel, if appropriate.

- Collect and confirm as many facts as you can.

- Assess risks and opportunities, and consider all audience groups (impacted, close to the impacted, nonimpacted, etc.).

- Determine the appropriate level and method of response. The worse the news, the more in-person you should be.

- Develop a communication plan targeting what you want each audience to know and do. Then assign resources and establish deadlines and guidelines to implement your plan and measure its effectiveness.

- Activate your communication plan, using outside consultants if needed.

- Debrief after the crisis passes. Find out if you got the outcome you wanted. That's the only way to know for sure that your plan was successful.

Visit truperception.com/thetruthabout to download a crisis management guide

Bill hadn't done any of these things until we met. But he learned quickly that without valid talking points and expert counsel, his emotions (and ego) would have derailed all his efforts, put his reputation at risk, and possibly cost him his company.

Thankfully, none of that happened. In fact, Bill spent the next eighteen months learning even more from me about how to effectively communicate across all aspects of his life and business. And when we parted ways, he said, "Melissa, I must admit: before I met you, I had no idea there was a way to tell the hard truth about business and not suffer horrible consequences. I always knew I should tell the truth; I just didn't know I could do it and still get results. You changed all that for me."

You see, Bill learned the truth about scandal. He realized he wasn't at the mercy of his circumstances and that he could come from a position of power and influence others, even in the most difficult situations. All he had to do was make sure his messages included an element of truth, consideration, and objectivity. That's where power comes from!

Throughout this book, you will learn how to create your own truth-filled *power phrases* so you'll never be caught off guard, have to guess at what to do or say in a crisis, or know how to respond when others try to sabotage you. Plus, I'll show you how easy it is to build power phrases over time, house them in a copy bible, and never be at a loss for words again.

It doesn't matter whether you're responding to haters, addressing skeletons in your closets, or trying to get your team to change: the truth will set you free. I know that from experience.

Chapter 1
The Truth about You

There I stood, in the middle of a conference room full of accountants. I was conducting a workshop on how to create a compelling elevator speech. As part of the process, I had them write a draft and then share it with the group. Without fail, each person started out by saying something like, "Okay, I didn't have much time to work on this" or "Mine isn't very good." Then they proceeded to rattle off what they had written, pausing periodically to insert more disclaimers, some as disheartening as "I'm terrible at this."

After three or four people read their drafts, I stopped the group, drew attention to their perhaps unintentional self-denigration, and insisted that everyone try again.

Whether it's rooted in humility or low self-esteem, many leaders take themselves out of the running before they're out of the gate. The intention seems to be to lower expectations so that it won't be a big deal if they fail.

The truth about you, if you're like most professionals, is that you're afraid. Fear of failure, rejection, and dissent are the most common fears I see, and it goes for anyone who's ever done any of the following:

- Started a presentation with an apology

- Told their team they're sleep deprived and not up to par

- Downplayed their individual contributions as being a team effort

- Insisted on making decisions by group consensus so everyone is culpable for mistakes

- Waited to share bad news to avoid perceived repercussions

Fear can get the best of us, especially when we're faced with harsh circumstances. That's the thing about scandal: it has a way of stirring up our most volatile, reactive emotions. And when the going gets really tough, most of us want to run because doing nothing can feel like the best course of action.

Big mistake. Scandal rarely resolves itself. What you need to do is stand strong and brave so that you can face the music.

My email and voicemail constantly fill up with requests from clients who need help managing conflict. The situations vary. Some clients want to know how to deliver bad news; others are trying to avoid a lawsuit. Regardless of the specifics, there's always a company reputation or personal brand at risk—and with that comes fear. The most common lament I hear during a crisis is, "I can't do this. I'm not strong enough. Maybe if we wait, it will work itself out."

Unfortunately, waiting often means disaster. That's what could have happened for one of my clients, Meg, who was asked to critique her boss to her boss's boss. Meg had been working for the same company for seventeen years. In all that time, she had been managing her boss, Mike, trying to get him to work her people less savagely. She constantly had to juggle his demands with her team's fatigue. She had done well enough over the years, but they'd recently taken on a new client and the added hours and focus were putting her team at risk. Plus, her health was starting to fail. The years of stress, anxiety, and sleep deprivation were taking their toll.

The entire office steamed like a pressure cooker that was about to blow. The good news was the company had just hired a brand-new director, who Meg's boss reported to. He had come in like a breath of fresh air, asking for feedback and offering reprieve. The only problem? Meg's amnesty would come at a high cost. Her testimony about her badly behaved boss would not be anonymous. In fact, Mike would receive a verbatim transcript of her review.

Meg was terrified. She was certain a candid review of Mike would damage their relationship. Either his feelings would be hurt, or he would be mad. The guilt over the years she'd remained quiet about his leadership style weren't helping. And the enormous underpinning of fear that he might retaliate threatened to derail all her efforts to save her team.

Doing nothing simply seemed like the safer bet. Unfortunately, doing nothing meant lying. And even though she knew she shouldn't, Meg wanted to lie. She wanted to say Mike was great, because then all those fears would go away. I knew she was guaranteed to suffer more if she lied, and I encouraged her to tell the truth. I promised her that if we created a message that told the director the truth about what was going on, without condemning her boss, she and her team would be the better for it. The right balance was essential.

So here was the question from her boss's boss. "What are some areas where Mike can improve?"

And this is the message I crafted for her to use: "Mike is committed to customer satisfaction in a way that's inspiring and full of integrity. At times, his ability to assess our intense workload is skewed by that devotion."

This message is honest, to the point, and considerate. It says that Mike has the right intentions, but he's still overworking his people. The idea was to help Mike feel the sincerity of Meg's compliment while still getting down to the truth. And it worked. Within a few weeks, Meg's team had the help they needed, Mike admitted his shortcomings, and Meg got the first good night's sleep she'd had in years.

The truth for Meg—and for you—is that fear doesn't have to win. You can maintain a favorable reputation, preserve relationships, and get results. However, you must overcome the second truth about you—thinking you can wing it.

Over the years, I've worked with too many leaders who were adamant that what they said and how and when they said it wasn't a big deal. When situations that called for tough tactics arose—like letting someone go—they thought that, if they just crossed their fingers and hoped for the best, their words would land favorably on their recipient.

Amateurishness can blow a chance to demonstrate the kind of business diplomacy that makes positive impressions, and ignoring the fact that you're on the stage of public opinion will not save you. If you try to fake your way through any presentation, you'll meander off track into tedium town and the tomatoes will fly. Or, worse, you will say the wrong thing and be subjected to harsher criticism. Remember when in March 2003 the Dixie Chicks' lead singer, Natalie Maines, made a derogatory comment about President George W. Bush? The subsequent media backlash brought their skyrocketing career to an immediate halt.

Whether you're afraid of failure, like my group of accountants, or retaliation, like Meg, winging it is never the answer. To help you overcome these truths about you: there's the copy bible.

Copy Bibles Are the Answer

Copy bibles contain precrafted messages to use online, in person, and over the telephone to promote yourself.

Their primary elements are a mission statement, a vision statement, an elevator speech, and polished responses to critical and controversial topics in your business or life—known throughout this book as power phrases.

- Your mission statement explains how the world would suffer if you didn't exist. It should inspire others to take action—to select your services, seek employment with you, and talk positively about you.

- Your vision statement describes where you're going and what you're going to achieve. It should be compelling, aspirational, and measurable.

- Your elevator speech should clearly articulate in short phrases what it is that you do and how others can benefit from knowing and working with you. It should include evidence that you can accomplish what you say you can.

- Your power phrases are short, practiced messages that help you manage uncomfortable situations, such as making a mistake, letting someone go, or raising prices. They also help you take advantage of opportunities, such as securing meetings, closing sales, and motivating your team.

The Benefits of a Copy Bible

All professionals who care about their personal identities should invest time in creating a copy bible. These pre-crafted messages build and protect your personal brand and ensure that you

- Come from a position of power

- Influence positive perceptions

- Communicate with confidence

- Have the precise language to deal with any kind of ambush, personal attack, or controversial issue

- Determine in less than ninety seconds if you're talking to a prospect

- Close even the most complex deals in the first meeting

Visit truperception.com/thetruthabout to download your copy bible template

I was introduced to the concept of a copy bible years ago, when I worked for Maytag. At that time, the company was one of the most recognizable brands in the appliance industry. Maytag was known to consumers as the dependability provider. Their company mascot—Old Lonely, the repairman who had no work because Maytag appliances were so durable—had convinced consumers everywhere that Maytag washers and dryers wouldn't break.

Whenever we launched a new product, we built a copy bible. It was comprised of the approved brand statements that employees and vendors were to use during trade shows, media events, and everyday sales conversations. All consumer-facing employees were required to learn the phrases within the copy bible so that they would be ready to explain how the product worked and what its benefits were.

Over the years, I adapted this concept. Anytime executives fumbled over what to say, when to say it, and how to say it, I sat them down and wrote their copy bible. Ideally, we'd revise the copy bible at least annually, if not monthly or quarterly.

In all of my time working for CEOs and business leaders, I have found that about 80 percent of the objections and issues that someone can throw at you are foreseeable. All your responses to these issues can be precrafted, stored in your copy bible, rehearsed regularly, and refined continually. It's an internal vault of content that can be drawn from when crafting any speech or email or even having a conversation with a client, prospect, or employee.

Copy bibles help you overcome a range of fears—from simple ones, like how to talk about yourself at a party, to the complicated ones, like what to do when lying seems like the better choice. And regardless of your fear, copy bibles always protect you from winging it.

When You Don't Have a Copy Bible

One summer night, I attended a casual open house where everyone seemed to lose sight of their communications compasses. They clearly had no copy bible when I said, "Tell me about yourself," because they all replied with the same wrong question: "What do you want to know?"

In effect, these well-intentioned people saddled me with the burden of discovery, assuming that I'd care enough to dig deeper. And that's a risky assumption. If they wanted to promote themselves or their businesses, or even just come off as interesting people, they needed to decide what they wanted me to know about them, not the other way around.

Had they invested time and effort into a copy bible, even if they weren't in the mood to prospect or promote, they still would have made a strong first impression. After all, you never know who you might meet.

Any of the following elevator speeches, all of which should be in your copy bible, would have sufficed:

- **Tongue-in-cheek:** "I'm an eager-to-please business owner."

- **Casually confident:** "When executives need to know how to talk, they call me."

- **Flying under the radar:** "I'm mommy to two adorable kiddos."

Some of these options afford more business opportunities than others. Either way, they demonstrate confidence and self-assurance, two characteristics all professionals should aspire to.

When Your Referral Partner Gets the Shaft

Here's another scenario: Let's say you get a new client based on a referral from a colleague. Your colleague was also hoping to be selected by the client, but they aren't chosen and you know it. To make matters worse, your new client hasn't shared the bad news with your colleague.

Unfortunately, the default message often goes like this: "I don't know what happened. Last I heard, they were still considering both of us. Maybe give him a call later this week. Thanks for the referral. I feel kind of bad about this. I swear, if it were up to me, every client would use you."

Even if the news is hard to deliver, be proactive whenever possible and always tell the truth. Omit emotional expressions and don't overpromise. If business complexities prevent you from delivering on your promises, your esteem will suffer.

A better message to have in your copy bible sounds like this: "Hi, Melissa, I hope all is well. I'm not sure if Pete has communicated the most recent developments on the project, so I thought I would reach out to you. My goal was of course for us to work together on this project, but it looks like they've decided to go with another marketing firm.

"My understanding is they saw a better cultural fit with the other firm. It's an honor to be serving this client, and I know I have you to thank for the opportunity. I will continue to advocate for you with this client and all other prospects whenever possible. Please let me know if there is anything else I can do."

Trust me, winging it always comes back to bite you in the end.

When You Wait Too Long

Brent, a client of mine, had started his business ten years before we met. He came up with a name for his company, printed some business cards, and started selling. Fast-forward to the present day, and out of nowhere, one of Brent's products was picked up by a local media outlet. The story spread so quickly that within a week Brent was on a plane to New York City for a live television broadcast.

Brent was in a panic when he called me. He hadn't expected to be in front of millions of prospective clients and potential employees, and he was not confident in his story. Because he'd never taken the time to craft a copy bible, this huge audience opportunity was a nightmare, not a dream come true. The scrambling we had to do in the seven short hours before his first-ever television debut was stressful and unnecessary. Trial by fire can work, but it's much more enjoyable to avoid the burns and get the blessing.

Remember, if things are going well for you, take advantage of the moment by thinking ahead: use any crisis-free time to craft and rehearse the right messages for every imaginable situation, whether good news or bad—before you need them. And don't let someone else tell your story for you.

When You Need Help

When my daughter was about six years old, she had a dilemma that had the power to negatively affect her life forever. So I put a stop to it. Here's what happened:

Every time she and I encountered a stranger or an acquaintance out in public, she would withdraw. No matter how much they coaxed and praised her, she wasn't willing to talk and wouldn't agree to high fives or hugs. The people we were with would laugh and tell her, "It's okay. You're shy." Even though I knew these people meant well, I didn't want anyone telling my daughter who she was.

So I always proclaimed the following: "She's not shy. She's reserved. She waits to see if the people she encounters can be trusted or not. This is very wise." My public affirmations not only increased my daughter's confidence but also gave her permission to be exactly who she was, without compromising her beliefs or trying to please others. It's hard to own your identity when others try to define you.

Words are powerful. They can build us up or tear us down. When we're hit with negative words, we tend to either strike back with indiscriminate force or sneak away to nurse our wounds in private. Unfortunately, neither of these reactions presents us in a positive light. They may even damage our reputations and careers.

How we manage our reactions to stressful situations makes a world of difference—to us and our reputation. My group of accountants learned to do exactly that after I stopped them from self-denigrating. I told them, "I get it. It's tough to promote yourself, especially when you're under pressure. But if you don't advocate for yourself, who will? So rather than shooting yourselves down, at least remain neutral about your efforts."

I gave them the following power phrases to try:

- "I have a draft to share."

- "I'd be delighted to go next."

- "I'm excited to hear everyone's feedback on
  my content."

No matter how afraid or prone to winging it you might be, there is hope. Simply craft your copy bible in a way that's truthful, considerate, and objective, and you'll never be at a loss for words again.

Knowing the truth about yourself and how to overcome these struggles is crucial to successfully preventing scandal. But it doesn't stop there. You also have to know the truth about "them." The truths about your opponent may seem harder to recognize, but they're not. They're actually so intrinsic to humanity that, in all the years I've been sharing them with leaders, not one person has ever disputed their validity.

Chapter 2
The Truth about "Them"

t was 1998, and I was a senior in college intern-ing for a leadership development company in Fayetteville, Arkansas. I don't remember anything that company taught me, but I will never forget the lesson I learned during a meeting with a client of theirs from Walmart.

Dan was unbelievable. He was the most impressive leader I had ever encountered. When he spoke, people listened. He never seemed to be out of sorts and always knew exactly what to say. On the day of the meeting, Dan had control of the floor, and we were having a pro-ductive discussion. Out of nowhere, an attendee named Bob took over and started lamenting everything under the sun. He used profanity, made demands, acted rudely, and hijacked the entire meeting.

As a young college student, I was shocked and clueless about what needed to happen next. I thought for sure Dan would yell at Bob and tell him to be quiet. But that's not what happened. Quite the contrary, in fact: Dan spoke favorably about Bob. He used a calm voice and kept his mannerisms composed, and in a matter of moments, he shifted the entire dynamic in the room from chaos to clarity.

Back then, I didn't know anything about handling high-pressure moments, but Dan did—and as I watched him, I decided that I wanted to be just like him. He inspired productivity, and he got us all back to work quickly.

Dan knew something none of the rest of us knew. He knew the truth about "them." He knew what it was that made his opponent tick. You see, in order for Bob to listen to Dan, Dan knew he had to convey two things: That he cared about Bob as a person and that the work Bob was doing was valuable.

The first principle is based on the theory of perceived organizational support, which I learned about in graduate school the next year. The theory was originally conceived by Linda Rhoades and Robert Eisenberger, and it says that employees work harder if they believe the company they work for cares about them. If they don't believe that, they won't work as hard—and might not work at all.

In my experience, this theory holds true for prospects, colleagues, vendors, friends, spouses, and even children. If people in your life believe you care about them as people, they are more likely to go down into the trenches with you. They will be more loyal and willing to form long-lasting relationships.

The second principle is likely also grounded in theory and supported by great volumes of research, but for me and most of my clients, it's just common sense. When you authentically convey that you care about people and that their work or presence matters, you will gain consensus sooner and get better results.

We often get tripped up when situations are complex and when perhaps we don't have a good answer. Maybe you don't know what an "I care about you" or "You matter" message sounds like. This is quite common, in fact.

But Dan knew, and now you will too.

Having worked in the field of communication all my life, I can tell you these messages are hugely important, but they're not rocket science. They're basically messages from a sender to a recipient using a particular vehicle—like your voice or an email—that is repeated often. And when you're finished speaking or writing, you should have successfully changed or reinforced a perception or behavior.

The key is authoring your message in a way that demonstrates that you care about your opponent and that he matters. That communication—clearly and consistently delivered in a caring and direct manner—is the answer. There's power in the words you choose and the way you deliver them. You, like Dan, can influence every single person you encounter—boosting productivity or changing or reinforcing a perception or behavior.

But, as I've already shared, it won't work if fear and unpreparedness are in control.

Overcoming Obstacles

Whenever I ask clients to tell me the one fear they have when it comes to addressing someone like Bob, they always answer the same way: "My biggest fear is the unknown, not knowing what's coming. How in the world am I supposed to prepare for an attack that I can't foresee?"

As I mentioned earlier, what you have housed in your copy bible will help you know what to say at least 80 percent of the time. But what about the other 20 percent?

When, out of the blue, someone attacks your character, usurps your authority (like Bob did), or asks a "gotcha" question, what do you say? The answer: Have a set of standard phrases on the tip of your tongue that you can use to buy time and disarm your attacker.

Dan had them. He used them that day in Arkansas, and I've been using them ever since. I call them power phrases, and they come in two forms: planned and immediate.

We've already talked a little about planned power phrases. They're what I gave my group of accountants to use when prefacing their draft elevator speeches and what I wrote for Meg to use with her bad-behaving boss. The premise for planned and immediate power phrases is the same. The main difference is you have time to create the former and the latter needs to be sitting on the tip of your tongue at all times.

Immediate power phrases typically consist of fewer words, and their primary purpose is to take you from a seemingly negative question or insinuation to a decisively positive message. They give you the power to turn hearts and minds around and set people on a path to accomplishing goals. Of course, to be effective, your power phrases must include truth, consideration, and objectivity.

Tell the Truth

Truth must reside somewhere in your power phrase. Although no two people are the same, and there are variances, men typically excel in this area; they are straight-shooters.

Women, on the other hand, often struggle with this element because they don't want to hurt anyone's feelings. Even though they want to tell the truth, they often cave and share a softer or completely evasive message.

Unfortunately, neither men nor women will get the results they want with this approach. And that's because just being truthful isn't enough. If you're unkind with the truth, people will resent you; if you're too soft with the truth, people will lose respect.

Be Considerate

Tell the truth, but in a considerate way.

This is the area where men often need a little polishing. They tend to employ the old-fashioned communication tactic that relies on "Look, I'm the boss, so you better do it." Those messages are ineffective: remember, no one will go down into the trenches with you if they don't believe you care about them as a person. Harsh demands are counterintuitive to influencing behavior.

Women tend to excel here. They're often more considerate and interested in preserving relationships, and never seem to run out of ways to soften the edges of a harsh message.

Remain Objective

Both men and women struggle with the third element: objectivity.

It's just too easy to forget the second side of the story. We're preoccupied with thinking either we're wrong or they're wrong. We rarely think it's possible that we're each a little wrong and a little right. However, when we take both sides of the bad news coin into account, we succeed in delivering a truly powerful power phrase.

Why? Because it's actually much harder to argue with someone who's already stated and eliminated your objection, and that's what talking objectively does. It says,

"Hey, this is my side, and that's your side. I know both of them, and I'm addressing them."

Politicians have been doing this forever. It dates all the way back to Aristotle.

Power Phrases

Here a few of my favorite power phrases:

- I don't know if that's an accurate characterization.

- Right now, we need to focus on this issue.

- I need your help to clear up a potential misunderstanding.

- Not exactly; let me explain.

- I understand that timelines can shift, and perhaps I haven't made my priorities clear.

- It's been my experience that the best approach for us is . . .

- It's too early to say for sure; let's talk about where we're at right now.

- I can't speak to all of that, but here's what I can tell you.

When you break each of these power phrases apart, you'll see where each one either implies or states truth, consideration, and objectivity.

What if Bob had said to Dan, "Dan, you totally screwed up the entire project"?

If Dan responded with, "I don't know if that's an accurate characterization," he would be implying truth while disagreeing with Bob. At the same time, he'd be considerate. He wouldn't be outwardly accusing Bob of attacking his character. He'd show him that he feels Bob's opinion matters even though he doesn't agree.

He'd also be implying objectivity. When he says, "I don't know if . . ." he's giving Bob the benefit of the doubt. He's implying, "You know, it's possible; I suppose it could be an accurate characterization. You may be right, but I may be right as well." This phrase is truly powerful. Dan's being considerate, telling the truth, and also offering a little objective wiggle room.

How about, "I understand that timelines can shift, and perhaps I haven't made my priorities clear." Again, the truth is implied: "You're late, Mr. Client. You didn't get me what I needed," but you're off-loading the blame to the ambiguous vacuum of time when you say, "timelines can shift."

This power phrase isn't pointing specific blame; it isn't so direct that it burns bridges. It's considerate and objective and takes some of the onus by saying, "Perhaps I haven't made my priorities clear, but I'm going to now."

Visit truperception.com/thetruthabout to download more power phrases

Benefits of Power Phrases

You may be terrified by the thought of telling a client or colleague no. Or maybe you do okay managing minor crises but panic when things get controversial. The good news is it doesn't matter what side of the communication meter stick you land on. If you are battling any kind of client complexity or employee concern, you can get your message out, even in the most difficult situations, and preserve your reputation. All you need are a handful of power phrases.

These power phrases can change your life forever. That's because no other communications tactic is more suited to address the truth about "them." People want to know that you care and that they matter. When you speak the truth in a considerate and objective matter, you make the strongest "I care" and "You matter" statements possible.

Because the lines between public and personal communications have virtually disappeared, leaders can no longer afford to focus their strategic messaging efforts solely on quarterly earnings calls and public relations events. How you talk with and write to your employees, vendors, and colleagues determines how they'll relate to your customers. Every word you say has the potential to win or lose brand ambassadors. And that's why you need power phrases.

There are three specific benefits to using power phrases:

1. They buy you time.

2. They defuse the situation.

3. They show diplomacy.

Whenever someone comes raging at you, a power phrase will buy you time to think about your response. I coach my clients never to immediately say "yes" or "no"; use a power phrase instead to give yourself time to decide what you really want to say.

You can say something as simple as, "That's an interesting perspective. You know, I haven't given that any thought before now." The seconds it takes you to say it, especially if you enunciate carefully, might be all you need to scan your mind to access your next power phrase (hopefully one that's planned and housed in your copy bible).

Second, power phrases defuse the situation. In bad-news scenarios, someone is often coming at you with a bit of aggression. They might be shouting or throwing things. They might be emotional, even crying. The calmer you are and the more considerate and objective your responses, the better.

If an aggressive opponent hears you speaking eloquently, they won't be able to help but notice the vast difference between their own outlandish behavior and your put-togetherness. They will naturally bring themselves down to better match your demeanor. If you shout, they'll shout louder. If you speak reasonably, they are much more likely to do the same.

My favorite benefit of power phrases is that they show you as a diplomatic leader. When you use this technique, you're seen as calm, composed, and collected. You have it together. You don't have to jump in with an answer. You take your time and make sure that you're offering a thoughtful response.

That shows diplomacy, which is a sign of a true leader. Having even one power phrase on the tip of your tongue—even one as simple as "Not exactly; let me explain"—will show your diplomacy. And if you have several power phrases ready to go, then you're golden. Once you start using these power phrases and see how valuable they are, you won't be able to live without them.

Practice When Times Are Good

You have to prepare long before the ambush ensues, well in advance of the scandal or bad-news situation. You have to practice power phrases and anything else housed in your copy bible when times are good so that they will naturally roll off your tongue when times are bad.

If you can train yourself to use these power phrases, then when times are tough or somebody comes at you with "I can't believe you're late on the project," you'll be able to say, "First, let me clarify. The timeline shifted. I'll see where we're at and get back to you." That is the secret to crafting influential messages in the face of controversy, avoiding mistakes and blinders.

Before You Act …

No matter where the controversy is coming from—an employee, client, or friend—the truth about "them" is they need to know that you care and that they matter. You do this by having phrases that tell the truth in a considerate and objective manner stored in your copy bible and committed to memory. Rehearse them when times are good, and you'll deliver them naturally when times are bad.

Even when times are so bad that you find yourself in the middle of a crisis.

Chapter 3

The Truth about Crisis

It was a cool April morning when Shelly walked into the diner off Lyndale Avenue, where I sat waiting for her. I wasn't sure why she'd called the meeting. All I knew was that she'd gotten my name from a mutual friend—an attorney.

She was younger than me, but not by much. Her hair was blonde and swept down the middle of her back. The coat she wore had brightly colored buttons, and the scarf around her neck was tied in such a way I could hardly see her face. She walked straight to the table and immediately burst into tears. I put my hands over her still-gloved fingers and waited for her to regain composure.

Once she started speaking, her story spilled out like an avalanche. She and Jamal had been friends and colleagues for more than fifteen years. He was married and so was she. They'd just returned from a weeklong conference in Alaska, where drinking, socializing, and a little table dancing had occurred. They'd spent a lot of time together, and their primary activity had been flirting.

When I asked her to tell me more, she leaned forward, putting her arms on the table, as though she were about to tell me a secret. Her voice was barely audible when she said, "The setting was very romantic. I was overwhelmed, drinking, of course. And I know that's no excuse, but one night after all the meetings had ended, I called his room and asked if he wanted to *get together*."

She looked at me to see if I'd understood what she was implying, and I nodded for her to continue.

"He said he'd given that a lot of thought and even though he wanted to, he couldn't go through with anything like that. We hung up the phone and that was it. The rest of the conference was all business. When we got back home, Jamal asked me to lunch. As soon as I sat down, he started shouting, accusing me of taking advantage of him. He said I was trying to destroy his marriage and using my leadership position to coerce him into an affair."

"What happened next?" I asked quietly.

"Well, I flipped out. I said the first thing that came to mind. "Oh my God, you're right. I did all of that. I'm so sorry." She went on to explain that he stormed out of the restaurant with plans to have her fired, but not before drawing up sexual harassment and discrimination charges.

I told Shelly that Jamal's ambush had caught her off guard, and it was guilt that crafted those words she spoke. In less than ten seconds, she had sentenced herself to a felony when she'd actually only committed a misdemeanor.

Unfortunately, because we're human, the truth is that emotions run high. So when someone mistreats us or questions our character, we tend to fall apart. Had Shelly been aware of immediate power phrases and had a few on hand that she'd rehearsed during good times, she might have said, "Not exactly, let me explain." That would have bought her a little time, helped defuse Jamal's attack, and possibly averted the crisis.

But that's not what happened. For the next several minutes Shelly grieved her situation and lamented about Jamal's intentions. She asked herself and me a number of questions: "Why is he doing this? What does he stand to gain? Hadn't he pursued me too?"

The funny thing about intention is it's something we always want to know, but it's the least important issue in a crisis. The *why* behind Jamal's actions was irrelevant. The only thing that mattered was Shelly's next move. How could she protect her reputation, avoid losing her job, and manage future interactions with Jamal? By the look on her face, I could tell she had no idea. Well-intentioned leaders are often ill equipped to handle the communication complexities hidden beneath this kind of problem. What seems like the right move typically backfires, and lost ground cannot be recovered.

A better approach is one where leaders go straight to the source of knowledge and build allies. It's not easy, but it is possible if you stick to this golden rule: ignore your feelings and do what's right. For example:

- If somebody sends you a nastygram, cool your heels before responding.

- When name-calling commences, be positive, or at least neutral, about the person in question.

- If you're hurt, write a message to the offending party. But before you send it, revise it until it's a message you would want to receive if the tables were turned.

Emotions are your enemy during a crisis. When we're emotional, we can't think clearly, and if we succumb to our emotions at any point, we'll be forced to do damage control.

The truth about crisis is that you need a plan. Ideally, you're able to foresee when a crisis could occur and have a plan in the waiting. But normally, you have to spring into action as soon as you know the crisis has occurred. And that's just what I did for Shelly. I immediately set about crafting her copy bible, which included planned and immediate power phrases for her to use with her boss, colleagues, and the media in case they became involved. The planned power phrase I wrote for her proactive use went like this:

"At a retreat in Alaska, there was a misunderstanding. I asked an employee whom I have known for fifteen years to spend some time with me outside of the group setting. He declined, and we went back to work. Within a week, he expressed concern that my request was inappropriate. It was a misunderstanding. Jamal and I have been professional colleagues and friends for many years, and I am committed to resolving the situation amicably."

The planned power phrases I wrote for her defensive use to address specific accusations were:

"My intention has always been to promote a professional working relationship with Jamal. Because of what I perceived to be mutual attraction, I asked him to spend time with me. Once he made his professional boundaries clear, I honored that, and we went back to work."

Then I gave her immediate power phrases she could use to help block and bridge back to her planned power phrases.

Remember, immediate power phrases typically consist of fewer words, and their primary purpose is to take you from a seemingly negative question or insinuation to a decisively positive message—one of your planned power phrases.

These included:

- I can't speak to all that, but here's what I can tell you . . .

- It was a misunderstanding that has since been resolved.

- I wouldn't say that.

- Not exactly; let me explain . . .

I worked with Shelly for about six weeks. In that time, we were able to prevent charges from being filed and salvage her job. Plus, Jamal left the company voluntarily.

Every crisis is different, but the emotional outbursts that accompany them seldom are. A client once approached me after he was threatened with a lawsuit. His customer wanted a refund. However, because contractual obligations had been ignored, my client wasn't willing to issue a refund and had lost his temper and threatened to countersue. Once he realized the risk to his reputation that a public lawsuit would entail, he quieted down and called me.

He wasn't interested in continuing to serve the customer and did not feel a refund was warranted, but he also did not want to get sued. So my challenge was to come up with a planned power phrase that solved all those problems. And here's how it went:

"There appears to be a misunderstanding. The reason we have an established protocol, which we ask our customers to adhere to, is to prevent situations like this from occurring. I understand that timelines can shift and that you may have intended to follow the process, but refunds only apply if fees are paid within the terms of the agreement. I wish there were a mutually beneficial way to resolve this, but given the circumstances, I'm unable to offer a refund. If you'd like to discuss this in more detail, please feel free to call me. Otherwise, I'd be happy to see if I can refer you to another provider that might be a better fit."

My favorite part of this message is, "I wish there were a mutually beneficial way to resolve this." That's the objectivity. "I do wish that it could work out on your side of the coin and my side of the coin, but given the circumstances, it can't." That's the consideration. And then comes the truth: "I'm unable to offer a refund." There's no name-calling; there are no accusations. It's a professional and courteous kiss-off.

And this would have become enormously helpful if the customer decided to pursue a lawsuit. In this case, they didn't—but if they had, my client would have evidence of a diplomatic exchange of the way the agreement was supposed to go.

How to Build Your Copy Bible

When you know the truth about crisis—that emotions run high and a plan is the only way to survive—the copy bible looks more and more like your saving grace. But do you know how to build one?

Let's say a former client believes you to be the worst provider on the planet. They feel so strongly, in fact, they go on Yelp and write you up a terrible review. Later, a prospect is considering working with you. They read the statements your former client wrote and express concern. They say, "It looks like you haven't always had the best customer reviews. We're not sure you're going to be the right person for us to work with. We need this project to go flawlessly."

Maybe the review your former client wrote wasn't fair. Perhaps they fabricated some wrongdoing on your part because they disputed a bill. Regardless, your response is the exact kind of language you need to precraft in your copy bible.

And when you're drafting, follow these simple steps:

1. Be straight-out honest, just as harshly truthful as you possibly can be. Write about what they did and how unfair it was. Write about how you feel guilty that you may have dropped the ball. Get it all out.

2. Be sure to capture the facts. Who was involved, when and where did the situation occur, why did it occur, and what specifically is it you want others to believe about you as a result of the situation? Write plainly and as

if there are no consequences for how poorly it might be received.

3. Then, start to edit based on the following three elements, which you have heard before: truth, consideration, and objectivity. Begin with consideration because you've already covered the truth.

4. Ask yourself, "Okay, what can I write that would be more considerate of the others that were involved, including myself?" Soften the language and make it as considerate as possible to give everybody the benefit of the doubt.

5. Finally, make sure that, while you're telling the truth in a considerate way, you're also demonstrating both sides of the story. That's the objectivity. The client felt neglected and your company had the best of intentions; make both of you look as good as possible.

For detailed instructions on how to build your copy bible, visit truperception.com/thetruthabout to download good ways to deliver bad news

Before You Act...

In any crisis situation, it's essential not to hide from your employees, clients, or customers. Be proactive, not defensive. If it's not appropriate to respond, say, "We are gathering facts so that we can fully understand what has happened (or what needs to happen), and we will communicate more as soon as we can."

Crisis comes in all shapes and sizes. The one that seems to bite my clients (and even me) the hardest is the kind that's shaped like a slithering snake: sabotage.

Chapter 4
The Truth about Sabotage

The Great Recession forced many major US organizations to reduce staff drastically. In December 2008, my position at 3M was eliminated along with almost two thousand others. Back then, I was the in-demand "darling of corporate America." Everything I touched turned to gold . . . until the day it didn't.

It was a tough season. Many people, for the first time in their lives, started feeling lucky to have a job. So it was with great relief that I landed a director of communications role just twelve months later.

Unfortunately, unbeknownst to me, a snake lay still in the grass. My nemesis—we'll call her Faith—showed signs of ill intent on the first day of my employment, but it wasn't until our paths crossed during an executive retreat that I realized how diabolical she really was.

After I confronted her about her poor work ethic on the trip, Faith promised to retaliate if I didn't back down. True to her word, when I arrived back in the office, a number of employees filed in, one by one, to warn me that Faith was speaking badly of me. In a nutshell: she took a platonic business relationship I had with a male colleague and turned it into a sordid affair. Word had already gotten to my boss, and the entire office was hanging in the balance.

Here's the truth about sabotage: when we get bit, we want to bite back.

We're human, right? When someone jeopardizes our reputation, we get mad. We want to set the record straight and make clear that we can't be messed with. Unfortunately, a no-holds-barred attitude on expressing every emotion we feel will not spare us from conflict; it will attract it. Rather, we have to learn how to convey the truth without losing sight of tact.

If someone has done you wrong, it's okay to tell them. The key to success, however, is not that you tell them—it's *how* you tell them. Unfortunately, the truth about sabotage is that no one ever teaches us how to tell our saboteurs that they've wronged us—at least not successfully.

And if you're like most of my clients, you could be prone to any of the following problematic approaches:

- Asking your colleagues for details about what Faith is saying in order to catch her in a specific lie

- Asking your colleagues to tell everyone what Faith is saying isn't true

- Confronting Faith directly to accuse her of lying

- Going home early to hide under the covers

The first two approaches are inherently wrong because they go against what is true about "them." How could I show my colleagues that I cared if I dragged them into my conflict with Faith? If I accused Faith of lying, the chances were pretty slim that I'd get the result I needed— for her to confess and apologize, or at least stop.

And even though hiding under the covers sounds nice, it is the worst approach of all because it negates the truth about us: once we overcome our fears and learn that the truth will set us free, we cannot go back to cowering in the corner.

So what did I do? For starters, the minute my colleagues finished their initial statement about Faith's behaviors, I thanked them for sharing their concerns, quickly assured them that I would take care of the matter, and then shifted the conversation elsewhere. If they tried to steer us back to Faith, I repeated the same steps, saying:

"Thank you again for sharing your concerns. I understand this is difficult, and I want you to feel comfortable approaching me about any topic. I'll take care of the matter and will use discretion in my approach. Since you're here, though, let's talk a little about [project]. How are the porotypes coming?"

Each of these immediate power phrases had a purpose.

- "Thank you for sharing . . ." and "I understand this is difficult . . ." demonstrated my care and concern.

- "I want you to feel comfortable . . ." made it clear how much my colleagues mattered to me.

- "Will use discretion . . ." was especially helpful in showing colleagues they were not at risk of exposure.

- "Since you're here . . ." blocked us from going back to the Faith story.

- "Let's talk about . . ." bridged us to a new positive topic.

All of these phrases told the truth in a considerate and objective manner. They also helped me buy a little time, defuse the situation (at least for the moment), and show my colleagues they could trust me as a leader.

Avoid Emotionally Charged Words

As soon as the last person left my office, I got busy crafting my planned power phrase to use with Faith. I didn't include the question "Are you spreading rumors about me?" because the phrase "spreading rumors" is emotionally charged. It has a negative connotation and can trigger negative emotions in an opponent, causing them to shut down or react defensively. I needed Faith to open up to me and respond favorably. Emotionally charged words or phrases had to be avoided at all costs. I tell my clients to steer clear of emotionally charged words in everyday conversation so they'll be less likely to use them in the midst of a scandal. Emotionally charged words and phrases include *ax to grind*, *ramifications*, *inferior*, *irritated*, *shocking*, *hate*, *nasty*, and *crooked*.

Visit truperception.com/thetruthabout to download a list of emotionally charged words

I also didn't include this question because it's not open ended. It could only be answered with a "yes" or a "no." It's been my experience that when you ask a closed-ended question eluding to bad behavior, like "Did you do it?" the automatic response is "No!" If this had happened, Faith would have been caught in a second lie, making her even more prone to dig deeper into denial.

Open-ended questions always encourage dialogue. When a person has to speak in full sentences, they'll share more and will be more likely to tell the truth. To encourage that from Faith, I wrote the following planned power phrase: "I need your help to clear up a potential misunderstanding. It seems conversations are occurring about me and Aaron that aren't factual. What can you tell me about your participation?" Finally, I rehearsed the power phrase, called a meeting with Faith, and delivered it.

She immediately denied saying anything to anyone. But rather than present the evidence I had (how could I, when it would expose my colleagues?), I said, "I'm glad to hear that, and I trust there will be no more conversations about me and Aaron occurring."

And there weren't. There was never another word reported to me by anyone. You see, I'd called her bluff. I was willing to brave the tough conversation and show her I would protect my reputation without accusing her or throwing my colleagues under the bus. No, I didn't get a confession, but that really wasn't my primary goal. My goal was to get the stories she'd invented about me to stop, and they did.

When sharing a strong opinion, you must choose your words carefully, keep your tone neutral, and be prepared to give credence to your opponent. I wish it were the case, but the truth about sabotage is your opponent always has something to gain by destroying you. The trick is wasting as little time as possible on figuring out what they have to gain and as much time as possible on not losing what they hope to steal. That's how it went for a client of mine named Jill.

When a Smear Campaign Ensues

It was spring of 2013 and the Minnesota state legislature was about to vote same-sex marriage into law. Controversy ensued on both sides of the political spectrum and social media was all abuzz. Debates over what was right or wrong seemed to never end and brother was often pitted against brother.

In midst of all this chaos, Jill was folding laundry. She'd just finished a photo shoot the night before for a corporate client and was waiting for her only child to go down for a nap. Her plan was to edit images for an hour and then get a few minutes of sleep herself. She'd already silenced her phone, so there was nothing standing in the way of her success. Within minutes, the towels were folded, her son was cuddled up in bed, and she was knee-deep in her work.

Just then, a knock on the front door threatened to ruin everything. She rushed to the foyer and pulled the door open quickly, silencing the noise and revealing her neighbor's stricken face.

"Why aren't you answering your phone?" he demanded. "We've been calling you for hours."

"It's on silent. What's going on?"

"Your Facebook account is blowing up! Someone said something about you during the Senate debate and now people are all over your page calling you a bigot and an extremist and saying that you're a hypocrite."

"What?! Who's saying that?"

"I don't know, but you better get online."

Jill flew back into the living room, terrified to see if what her neighbor said was true and, if so, hopeful that no one but her small circle of friends had seen it. It only took two seconds to realize those hopes were in vain. Tons of comments filled her screen and none of them looked good.

One post in particular caught her eye. It was from a man named John, and it read:

> *"Hi Jill, I hope this message reaches you well and you're having a wonderful day. Today, during the Senate debate on same-sex marriage, one of the senators (the name escapes me) mentioned you performing photography services for his niece's wedding.*
>
> *In his speech, he stated that you are a deeply religious person, and if you were approached by a same-sex couple to perform photography services at their wedding, it would make you uncomfortable and you would suggest the couple find someone else to perform the services.*
>
> *My question to you: Is this true? I would like to believe that you're not a bigot, but I don't know and wanted to give you the opportunity to defend yourself. Thanks, John"*

She didn't know John and had no mutual friends with him, but no matter how quiet she tried to keep her mind, the word "bigot" kept screaming at her like a violent offender.

In an instant, she saw her future flashing before her eyes: clients dropping like flies, her bank account emptying down to zero, and all for what? She didn't even remember photographing a wedding for any senator's niece.

By the time I got to her house, she was in shambles. Once I'd calmed her down and asked a few quick questions, I wrote the first part of her copy bible. The following power phrase had to be written immediately, mainly to buy us time, but also to thwart any additional actions her opponent was planning.

> *"Hi, John, I was not aware that anyone referenced me or my company. Let me check into this, and I will get back to you soon. Thanks for the heads up."*

Remember the truth about sabotage: the senator had something to gain. John, the stranger who was trying to elicit a response from her, likely had something to gain too. We didn't know what it was. It could have been something as benign as curbing boredom or as self-serving as using Jill as a conduit for media attention. Either way, it didn't matter. The only thing that mattered was preserving Jill's professional reputation.

Regardless of your political, religious, or socioeconomic views, no one has a right to define you but you. Had Jill spoken for herself at the Senate debate, that would be one thing, but having someone else speak on her behalf, without her consent, was sabotage. And then having another person publicly accuse her of being a bigot was like being bitten by the same snake twice.

She needed to defuse the situation. So I had her wait several hours before posting the next part of her copy bible. This time we addressed the truth in a considerate and objective manner, casting everyone in as favorable a light as possible:

> *Hi John, I was able to confirm through a few sources that a senator did reference my company during Monday's debate. My understanding is that he admitted he was only making an assumption about me, which is good news.*
>
> *I'm a for-profit business, and aside from a client not agreeing to my rate, our schedules not syncing up, and there not being a stylistic fit, I'm not accustomed to turning down opportunities. Thanks for surfacing the issue, and feel free to message me if you have any other questions.*
>
> *Have a great day, Jill*

The result? John wrote back, "Thanks for your response, Jill! I appreciate your professionalism and respect! I wish you the best and much success." The media never got involved, and within a few days, Jill's Facebook page went back to normal.

Before You Act . . .

Remember that full disclosure and authenticity are *not* one and the same. You can be real—and tell the truth—without baring your soul. Practice moderation to avoid regrets.

No matter what, never bite the snake that bit you. He'll only strike back with more force. Know how to approach your opponent from a place of consideration and spare yourself the agony of trying to learn what they have to gain.

Avoid emotionally charged words at all costs, and before you know it, you'll have defanged every snakelike culprit in your midst. However, keep an eye out for the wolf in sheep's clothing known as change. Harmless as it sounds, change can turn into crisis, faster than you can say, "Little pig, little pig, let me in."

Chapter 5

The Truth about Change

Early in my career, I worked for a well-known manufacturing company. One day, seemingly out of
the blue, our CEO sent a company-wide email
announcing that our entire IT department was being
outsourced. In his message, he explained that impacted
employees would be rebadged to the new IT provider—
or terminated.

Because the CEO was smart and accomplished, I
believed he emailed this emotionally charged message to
thousands of employees for a good reason. I had no idea
what that could be, but I stayed naively loyal nonetheless.

After all, he looked like a harmless sheep to me.

Unfortunately, with each passing day, he proved himself to be a wolf who expected employees to kowtow to his demands. He repeatedly ignored proven methods on how to communicate major change and refused to solicit advice from experts. Inevitably, his poorly chosen and ill-timed words devastated employee morale, resulting in poor productivity and profit losses.

To make matters worse, it was only five years later that the company succumbed to a seemingly unwanted acquisition by its biggest rival and competitor. At the beginning of his CEO term, the company had a solid market share, strong profits, and a trusted brand. I venture to guess that he was singlehandedly responsible for the demise of the entire company.

His verbal and written blunders presented me with a case study in the dos and don'ts of effective change communications. In the years since that experience, I have learned that unless they are naturally gifted, someone really does have to show even smart and accomplished CEOs how to communicate well through change. When they do, people work harder and are more loyal to the company and its brand.

We'd all like to think we know how to communicate. But there are times when the news is so tough even the most eloquent speakers freeze. No matter what form the change comes in, if it's news your recipient doesn't want to hear, it becomes news you don't want to deliver.

Fueled by fears of how they'll be perceived, many bosses stammer, stutter, and blunder through major change announcements. That's why they often choose to hide behind political jargon or sneak out the back door after leaving a scary sticky note on your cube wall. Why? Because the truth about change is that nobody wants to be seen as the bad guy.

When You Don't Want to Be Seen as the Bad Guy

I remember the first time an executive asked me to bury his change message beneath a pile of buzzwords. He said, "Melissa, I want you to craft this message so that our readers won't have a clue about what we're telling them." He was so afraid of looking like a bad guy that he wasn't willing to be transparent.

It took me hours of explaining to help him see why such a request would result in CEO suicide. Fortunately, he saw the light and allowed me to craft an authentic message that offered his employees the dignity they deserved— and preserved his reputation.

If only the executive vice president of Microsoft, Stephen Elop, had received and heeded the same advice. Instead, he did the unthinkable: On July 17, 2014, he sent thousands of employees a heinously botched memo about pending job cuts and made himself the laughingstock of Internet news feeds and social-media posts everywhere.

What made Stephen's message so bad? First, people aren't stupid, and they know a pig wearing lipstick when they see one. No matter how many times a leader writes the words "strategy," "plan," and "focus" (thirty-nine times, for Stephen), readers aren't fooled. As quickly as you can say "corporate speak," they'll skim through every last piece of jargon until they find the truth, all the while cursing the name of the person trying to sell them an expired bill of we-care-about-you goods.

Rather than get to the point in the first sentence, Stephen's message rambled on for eleven paragraphs before he admitted, "We plan that this would result in an estimated reduction of 12,500 factory direct and professional employees over the next year."

His second and even more grievous error was his complete lack of humanity. In all 1,111 words, he never once referred directly to the reader. Shockingly, he never used the words "you" or "your." There was no mention of "how hard *you* worked" or "how valuable *your* contributions are" or even "how difficult this news must be for *you* to hear." Nothing. His message, in fact, read with such third-person indifference that it felt like an obituary written for someone with no friends or family. No one will go down in the trenches with you if the best you can do is lump all your hard workers into a nebulous "team" that gets shipped off the island without a personalized thank-you or goodbye.

And there was so much more he could have improved on, starting with choosing a better medium, such as an in-person information cascade, in which each level of management informs the employees underneath them. But until this leader faces his fear of being seen as the bad guy, it won't matter if he sends a singing telegram; he'll still be at risk of failing.

Stephen likely meant well. It's been my experience that leaders often do. Yes, there are some wolves out there, but the majority are well intentioned. They lose sleep at night and are near tears when survey results come back reflecting low morale or approval ratings.

Bad News Needs to be Delivered In Person

But unfortunately, they don't know what to do when change occurs. They don't know how to communicate well. And Stephen, like many leaders, had fallen for the lure of email as a primary mode of communication. After all, it's easy to hide behind the cyber wall when bad news has to be delivered, because not only do you protect yourself from having to watch someone suffer through a potentially painful experience, but you also get to pretend you're not a bad guy after all. But the truth about change, especially if it's negative, is that it requires in-person delivery whenever possible. Here's why:

- It demonstrates courage—a desirable trait in any leader.

- You have more control of the message.

- A conversation affords the impacted party the most dignity.

- Everyone has an opportunity to speak their piece.

- Tone of voice and nonverbal communication can complement your words and reinforce the intended message.

Stop Change from Turning into a Crisis

If you can't personally deliver bad news because of the size of your audience, consider a video message, telephone conversation, or broadcast voice mail. Email should be your last resort. The worse the news, the closer to in-person you should be. And if you want to protect your change from turning into crisis, follow these simple, in-person steps:

Step 1: Deliver the worst part of the news first. In other words, rip the bandage off. For example, if you're reducing headcount, say, "I have some difficult news to share with you. Your position is being eliminated, effective today."

Step 2: Offer any semblance of good news. In other words, once the bandage is off, apply medicine immediately by saying, "Let me walk you through your severance package and options for continuing your health insurance."

Step 3: Provide the reason why. Only after your listener knows how the change will impact their livelihood are they able to hear you anyway. One example is to say, "For the past six months, I've been evaluating performance. In order for us to meet budget, I've had to make the difficult decision to reduce our headcount by 5 percent."

The same steps apply whether you are downsizing, have lost a huge client, have to give someone else the promotion, or don't want to work with a certain vendor.

Most of the leaders I've encountered try to pull the bandage off in a slow, agonizing fashion like Stephen. They do this by either avoiding the conversation altogether or by offering so many background details that the impacted employee suffers a mini stroke waiting for the big bad wolf to blow their house down.

Show your people that you care about them and that they matter. Tell the worst news first, offer any good news you may have, and then provide context. You should also have a few power phrases in your pocket to block and bridge back to message, such as:

- I know this is difficult.

- It is never easy when business decisions result in [job loss, budget cuts, loss of contracts].

- I wish I were sharing different news.

- I can't speak to all that; here's what I can tell you . . .

- Right now, we need to focus on . . .

During every bad-news moment, there is the potential for crisis. Tensions are high, and your listener may flip out—but that's not the only time change can turn into crisis. Often there is a silent crisis *before* the bad-news moment, one you can't see until it's too late. The truth about change is if you're not communicating, your people aren't working.

No News Isn't Always Good News

Over the years, the most common problem I've seen with change communication is that leaders wait too long to build a formal communications plan. They tell me they will be communicating at some point; they're just not ready yet. I tell them the same thing every time: just because you're not shouting the message from a loudspeaker doesn't mean your employees can't hear you. Then I ask a few probing questions:

- How many closed-door meetings have you had in the last month?

- How tense is your posture or facial expression in the office?

- How many of your current staff members know about the upcoming changes?

- How easily do you suppose they are sleeping at night?

- How many projects or product launches have you or they arbitrarily put on hold?

When they give me the same answers I've heard hundreds of times before, I share a little bad news with them. You see, at no time are productivity levels more at risk than during layoffs or leadership shake-ups. And the more closed-door meetings or project halts you have, the more likely it is for negative buzz to infect water-cooler conversations.

Employees do their best work when they can see how their individual efforts contribute to the company vision. If that vision seems compromised, they have nothing to anchor their efforts to and will—perhaps unconsciously—lengthen their lunch breaks, browse a little longer online, and engage in gossip.

Here's how you avoid these pitfalls:

- Have a plan. Train your leaders so they know how to conduct themselves before, during, and after decisions have been made and change has occurred.

  Visit truperception.com/thetruthabout to download the change communications plan

- Speak objectively. Avoid talking about employees working for the company "forever." You're better off saying, "We have to do what's best for our business, customers, and team."

- Empower people to be the CEOs of their own lives. It's limiting for them to rely solely on one job or company for their long-term livelihood.

- Stay positive or at least neutral.

Change Doesn't Have to be Hard

Because the truth about change is it doesn't have to be hard. Leaders, I understand why you regularly say "change is hard" when you're addressing your team about a switch in policy, procedure, or practice. You're trying to show that you're thinking about them, that you're putting yourself in their shoes, and that you realize that the road ahead may not look the same as the road just traveled. But you are not doing anyone any favors by saying "change is hard." In fact, it's a disservice.

Change is the act of making or becoming different. There's nothing positive or negative about it. It all depends on your perspective. For example: when the Vikings shocked us by winning in the 2018 playoffs, we cheered, even though this wasn't what we fans were used to seeing. But that same change led to disappointed Saints fans.

Prefacing a communication about change by asserting how difficult it may be is one of the worst things you can do. For example, let's say you recently announced that your company is being acquired by a larger company. Chances are, your staff is mighty anxious. They are worried about losing their jobs, their autonomy, or the company's culture. Saying "change is hard" just fuels this anxiety.

Sure, your intent is right. Workers need to know that they are more than just Monopoly properties being bought and sold around a giant game board. During transitions, it's important that leaders reassure their teams and show them that they care and that their work matters. This knowledge is what fuels productivity as well as creativity. That's why experienced leaders bring in communication consultants during transitional times.

Leaders, however, also need to give workers some credit and stop with the "change is hard" rhetoric. Most professionals understand business. They understand that sometimes you need to sell a product line, restructure, or merge to stay profitable.

Instead, leaders need to explain the benefits of the change. They need to keep the emphasis on the positive, rather than repeating a pessimistic phrase and feigning understanding. They need to be clear that change can bring good and, most importantly, include specific ways that individuals can contribute. This positivity creates a culture that embraces change and that makes transitions a lot easier.

Whether you change or not has less to do with who you are and more to do with how you're being dealt with. In other words, it comes down to how a person communicates with you.

One thing I can say for sure from my years in communications is this: communication and change are positively correlated. When you receive the right messages, you are more likely to change. Likewise, the better you are at communicating with others, the more likely they are to change.

How to Instill Change in Others

The trouble is, very few people understand this. Instead they resort to detrimental communication tactics like casting blame, making threats, or using negative reinforcement (e.g. "you never" or "you always" statements). Trust me, this approach doesn't work. If you want to instill change in others—or in yourself—follow these techniques instead:

- **Keep it positive.** Change is an uphill battle, so take a cue from *The Little Engine That Could.* Phrases such as "piece of cake" and "you got this" will go a long way in helping others see that change is possible.

- **Chunk it down.** The smaller the change, the easier it is. When dealing with long-term changes, break them down into shorter, doable increments. For example, say, "Let's build a seven-day plan, see how much we're able to accomplish, and then revisit it next week."

- **Praise the effort.** It takes time to truly change. The more encouraging you are, the better. Messages like "I see how hard you're working," "You're getting stronger every day," and "Thank you for making such a conscious effort" will up the ante and bring results sooner.

- **Offer public praise.** There is no better change motivator than recognition, and the most effective kind of recognition is a third-party compliment. For example, telling a friend how impressed you are by your son's change efforts and letting him overhear is a much more effective form of recognition than telling him directly.

- **Focus on benefits.** People resist change because they fear the unknown or believe they will lose something of value. Clearly telling them how much better off they'll be when the change occurs is the best line of defense against resistance.

Of course, with job loss, you have to tread lightly. However, hope can always be implied through your recognition of efforts and an optimistic tone of voice. You can't force people to change. But if they're open to it, they respond better to a positive communication style that makes change easier, quicker, and more sustainable.

Before You Act...

Regardless of the potential for bad news in any employee-employer relationship, don't be afraid of being seen as a bad guy. Don't forget, there are two truths about "them" that everyone in a leadership or management role should know: people want to work for a company they believe cares about them as individuals, and employees need to believe that the work they're doing matters. When you are mindful of these two truths, which get to the heart of what makes people tick, talking with employees about change becomes easier—and more effective.

Get in front of your people and spill the truth as quickly as possible; save the strategic explanations for later, when your audience is more likely willing to listen. Speak in plain English and be considerate, taking time to connect with your audience and thank them for a job well done. Your productivity levels and reputation as a leader depend on it.

The truth about change is it doesn't have to be hard. Oh, how I wish that were true of the next type of crisis—haters. The truth about haters is they're worse than all the snakes and wolves in the world. They're nasty, two-headed trolls. But don't worry, there is hope.

Chapter 6

The Truth about Haters

Our world is plagued with haters. Allegations of police brutality, racial injustice, and wrongful deaths run rampant. Given this emotionally charged environment, dissent is bound to occur. Recently, on a social media feed, I witnessed one firsthand.

In reference to an article about a college hosting a "no-whites-allowed pool party," one user wrote, "*Maybe they'd feel even more comfortable if they had their own drinking fountains and lunch counters . . .*"

To which his friend replied:

> "*We may have widely different views, but your comment above should go down as tasteless, insulting,*

and frankly—irresponsible. I'm disgusted you'd be so flippant about America's troubled past in the civil rights era. Your racism is showing."

These are the exact kind of conversations I am so inclined to engage in. However, I rarely do. I still remember the first time I thought my diplomatic gifts could neutralize a heated situation. I was a teenager caught in the middle of a brawl between a friend of mine and a stranger in a back alley of Ottumwa, Iowa. Both young men were reckless, fierce, and hell-bent on destruction. I tried to intervene with reason, empathy, and humor, but the violence escalated.

This incident ranks as one of my worst life experiences. Luckily, everyone survived. But I was forever changed. I knew for certain that I never wanted to be in the middle of that kind of hate-filled conflict again. Not only because of the trauma that came with it, but also because I realized that I should have saved my breath instead of trying to fight a battle I couldn't win.

It's the same in business and on social media. We often find ourselves trying to fight when the chances of us winning—of changing a person's mind or inspiring a positive outlook—are slim to none. The truth about haters, unlike those who try to sabotage us, is that most of them have nothing to gain. They're simply out to get us.

I saw this with an up-and-coming young woman who presented at a business conference in the Twin Cities. During her talk, she made reference to an insult she had received after being rewarded a substantial, highly coveted grant. The demeaning comment went something like this: "Nowadays, all it takes to get promoted is a short skirt and bright red lipstick."

When Haters Attack Your Character

While this was disheartening to hear, it's not the first time spiteful words have been used in a professional context. For me, it happened in 1999, not long after starting my first corporate job. I had just had the pleasure of enduring my first-ever performance review. My manager (we'll call him Tim) had already accepted a new position within the company but was pulled back temporarily to cofacilitate my review with his replacement. I don't remember the overall rating Tim gave me, nor the whopping salary increase I'm sure I *didn't* receive, but I'll never forget what he said. Near the end of the tag-team critique, he summed up my abilities and contributions this way: "Melissa, you're pushy, aggressive, and overbearing."

Because I had never heard these words used to describe me, I was shocked. However, I did my best to maintain my composure—and then turned the tables. "Can you give me an example of a time when you've seen me being pushy, aggressive, or overbearing? I just want to make sure I understand how these characteristics are affecting my performance."

"No," he replied, "it's just a general observation."

Call it intuition (or youthful stubbornness), but I decided right then that his inability to provide a concrete example meant that he just didn't like me. He wasn't trying to help; he was being mean.

It wasn't possible for his hater, troll-like behavior to be self-serving because he had already left the department. Our professional interactions were over, and no one was holding him responsible for my actions anymore. All he wanted to do was hurt me. This beautiful realization gave me the freedom to neutralize his otherwise piercing comments and take them in stride. So I told him, "Let me know if you see this behavior in the future. That way I'll be able to assess my actions and make job-related improvements." And that concluded my review.

When Haters Vandalize

A more aggressive incident happened to a CEO client of mine, Rick, when his company's property was vandalized—not once but twice in the same day. I was about to leave for a scheduled meeting with Rick when I received a text from his CFO, Jeanne. Jeanne was distraught and looking for feedback from me. Here's what she wrote:

> *"Last night, during second shift, someone jammed up the air conditioning. It broke, and it was so hot that the whole entire plant had to be shut down until it was fixed. It was a nightmare. The second shift supervisor reported it to Rick, and he spoke to all employees about it during the shift change. I thought Rick did a great job of addressing the issue, but within two hours, it happened again! I'm at a complete loss. Please help!"*

I knew exactly why it had happened again, and I told Jeanne to meet me in Rick's office so I could explain. Once we were all together, I asked Rick to tell me what he'd said to employees during the meeting. Here's what he said:

> *"If anyone has a problem with me or the company, all you have to do is come and talk to me. It's not necessary to vandalize company property. This isn't cool. I'm here, and I'm always willing to listen. You don't have to do this. It's a giant waste of my time and everybody else's time, so knock it off."*

Just as I'd suspected. Rick had faltered in his communications approach. When he addressed all employees, he narrowed in on the wrong audience, speaking directly to the anonymous offender. Big mistake.

You see, the truth about haters is they're not your primary audience. For starters, you're not likely to change a troll's mind. They're often set in their ways, and no matter what you do or say, they're going to be against you. Vandalism is by definition the willful destruction or defacement of property for no reason other than to do something malicious.

Trolls and haters deserve grace and mercy like everyone else, but not at the expense of your reputation. It is quite common for a leader to speak to an anonymous offender in a large group setting. After all, how else are you going to get a message to them? The trouble is, you're ignoring the majority of people who would never consider defacing company property and sending an unwieldy message to them by mistake. Plus, anyone who might have been on the fence could easily be tipped into vandalism after such a public scolding, which is probably what happened.

So I told Rick, in the future, to always speak to the vast majority of employees who value company property.

And, of course, cast everyone in as favorable a light as possible. Say:

"I have news to share about an incident that occurred last night on second shift. Someone tampered with the air conditioning, rendering it unusable and causing production to stop temporarily.

"I recognize that nearly every single one of you in this room has a great work ethic and strong values and always treats company property just as you would your own property. I want to thank you for that. I trust this is a one-time event. I will be monitoring the area more closely and, if necessary, will increase security efforts. Because what's most important to me is that every one of you has a safe and comfortable work environment."

This message helps elevate offenders to a level of ethics shared by colleagues, lowers the chances of repeat offenses, prevents anyone who may be on the fence from toppling over, and reinforces the desired behaviors of nonoffenders.

I told Jeanne and Rick that unless they knew who the offender was and could have a private conversation, they needed to speak to the majority of their audience, who weren't involved. They were astonished but immediately saw how the message went astray. Rick agreed to weave these power phrases into his future messages, and the vandalism eventually stopped.

When Haters Take to Yelp

Just as the vandal wasn't Rick's primary audience, neither are haters on Yelp or other crowdsourced reviews yours. When one of my clients called me about a negative review her company had received, I told her that the response I'd craft would be written mainly for her satisfied clients and employees, not only for the one unsatisfied person who wrote the review.

Over the summer, she'd worked with a temporary agency to bring on additional staff to help with an influx of projects. One such temp didn't have a favorable experience, and he voiced it online. Here's what he wrote: "Worst place I've ever worked with. The leader that ran [the project] was completely unprofessional and unreasonable in many ways. Mathew."

The bottom line in business is that we need people to be in agreement with us. If they're not in agreement with us about our personal integrity or our company brand, they're not inspired, working hard, promoting our products, or keeping customers happy. That's why it's important to address employee concerns as soon as possible. Unfortunately, when concerns are shared publicly, they're not always well intended.

However, others are watching you very closely, and how you treat a displaced employee is how they believe you'll treat them under similar circumstances. So always respond—at least once—to public reviews, addressing the author but, more importantly, addressing the rest of your audience. Here's how I did that for my client's message to Mathew:

> "Hi Mathew, my name is Mary Smith, and I am the CEO of [company]. I appreciate your feedback. My team and I are always interested in how to improve our company. I am happy to talk with you about your experiences while working for us through a temporary agency. You can reach me directly anytime at [email]. Thank you."

Now, had Mathew continued to vent about his experience unfavorably online, I would have written another message for Mary to take the conversation offline and instruct her to stop replying if it continued to escalate. We can't let troll behavior incite us. Your time is valuable, and once you have addressed the issue for the majority of your audience watching, you can disengage.

Protect Yourself from Haters

Unless a global communication transformation occurs, most of us can expect to encounter haters or trolls in the future. Accepting this painful fact of life is the first step to being prepared to successfully meet it head-on. Still, there are steps we can take to protect ourselves in abusive situations.

- **Never give anyone permission to mistreat you.** Don't allow yourself to be victimized in the name of niceness, and certainly not in the name of perception. Walk away, get off the call, or end the email chain as quickly as possible. By disengaging from an out-of-control situation, you demonstrate professionalism and self-respect.

- **Always stay focused on the positive.** Refuse to engage in mean-spirited hate talk. Save your energy for the things in your life and business that deserve attention.

- **Shake off those feelings of guilt.** You can't solve someone else's problems. It's their choice whether they want to get help for their issues or continue mistreating others. Don't hold yourself accountable for their dysfunctional behavior.

- **Take the bite out of their bark.** If someone discredits or condemns you, mentally flip their slight into an accolade. In other words, take what was said and translate it into a decisively positive thought. If they say you're a loser, tell yourself you just won an Olympic gold medal.

- **Offer a disarming comeback.** Have a handful of power phrases ready to go. Savvy professionals use this image-saving tactic to exude confidence under pressure. When the accusations fly, simply reply, "I wouldn't say that," "Here's what I can tell you," or "Not exactly—let me explain."

- **Don't stoop to their level.** Responding to slurs with more slurs can only result in an ugly confrontation. Instead, say, "Thanks for sharing your insights with me," and walk away.

Whether you're a CEO, individual contributor, or recent college grad, you can positively influence perceptions, maintain control of any conversation, and keep your emotions in check, even when encountering the antics of a hater on a power trip.

Before You Act . . .

The best defense is a good offense, right? Start by crafting some power phrases that can help you exit bad conversations gracefully. For example, "I prefer to think positively about this issue," or "I'd be happy to talk about this when you're in a mood to listen." Remember, you can tell the truth, be considerate, and be objective even when you're dealing with a hater or troll.

But not everyone who says something nasty is out to get you.

Chapter 7

The Truth about Mistakes

Some people are just young and dumb. That's how it was for me in the summer of 1994. I was nineteen years old, working as a trainer for a telemarketing company in southeast Iowa. We were hosting a train-the-trainer event in Cedar Rapids, and trainers from all across the state were in attendance, including me and my coworker Nate.

We'd only been at the event for three hours when I used—for the first and last time in my life—a racial slur, turning what had been the loveliest of times into a disaster of epic proportions.

I made my first mistake the moment we entered the bar. The entire team was waiting for us, and the welcome reception had already begun. Nate shouted hello to a few people he knew and then leaned in closely to whisper in my ear. "Do you want me to get you a drink?" he asked. "We can share it under the table."

I thought about that for a moment. What harm could a little alcohol do? Granted, I wasn't of age, but here I was for the first time in my semiprofessional career at an event with mature business people. I didn't want to look like a baby. "Sure, that sounds great," I replied.

I tried to take it slow, but before I knew it the room was spinning and I was making fast friends with everybody. However, one person stood out from the rest. Her name was Jasmine. I took one look at Jasmine, a mother of two, out on that dance floor, and I was smitten. To me, she was everything I was not—cool and confident—gliding across the floor like she hadn't a care in the world.

Janet Jackson's "That's the Way Love Goes" was playing. All eyes were on Jasmine as she coaxed me and Nate onto the floor. Eight songs later, we'd mastered every step of her routine. Together we nearly brought the house down. By the time the DJ stopped the music, the crowd had thinned to the three of us and a few other trainers. We laughed and talked and carried on for another hour. And when the sun finally set, we all started moving toward the door.

Once outside, Nate headed straight for the driver's side while Jasmine and I rounded the hood of my car. Nate said, "Give me the keys," and motioned for me to get in the back seat. The back seat: the place where less conversation would occur, the place where no radio choices were made. Of course, I would submit myself to the exile of the back seat. After all, I was the smallest, the youngest, and the least experienced, and I had been drinking underage. But more than anything, I wanted Jasmine to have the seat of honor. She had given me, to date, one of the best nights of my life, and it was the least I could do.

And right here is where I made my second mistake. For some reason, likely a mix of minor intoxication and significant insecurity, I tossed my head back in playful defiance and delivered a phrase I'd heard a million times before but had never once uttered. The first few words slid off my tongue like butter: "You're going to make me ride . . ." The last few oozed out in slow motion like black tar: "n*gger in my own car?"

As soon as the words escaped my lips, my brain connected what I'd said with what those words meant. All the ground I'd gained and the friendship I'd made with this stunning black woman were gone. It that one moment, my credibility was lost. I knew it and so did she. And oh, how I crumbled beneath the weight of that sentence. All the color draining from my contorted face and the words of regret spilling out faster than the last drink in my glass. I tried to justify my words but only tangled a tighter web around my tongue. In the end, she stormed away, hitching a ride with the other car, and I cried myself into a frenzy with Nate behind the wheel of my car.

If only the world would have opened up and swallowed me whole. But I wasn't that lucky. Instead, I spent the rest of the event avoiding Jasmine and letting Nate play interference between us. Shame had frozen my tongue forever, and no amount of his efforts to iron out the mess I'd made worked. He tried to talk me down from the ledge, but it was no use. Time was not a friend of mine, and I counted the minutes until I was finally released from the prison of my own making and we all went our separate ways.

All along, Nate tried to tell me the error of my ways. He said, "Melissa, you made way too big of a deal out of it. You should have laughed it off and made light of the whole situation. As soon as you flipped out, she did too." But I just couldn't comprehend how such an offensive phrase could have come from my lips.

Sadly, the truth about the tongue is no one can tame it. And the more I tried to analyze why I had said it, the further away I got from what mattered most—how I could undo it. All these years later, I can now say with absolute certainty what I should have done and said differently.

First, "I'm sorry" wouldn't have done the situation justice. That's because "I'm sorry" warrants negative connotations. Thanks to errant politicians, CEOs and celebrities resorting to scripted mea culpas, the world has become cynical about what an authentic apology even sounds like. So, even when you're in the wrong, saying "I'm sorry" can hurt you: It makes you—and the person hearing it—feel bad.

A better choice, and what I should have done with Jasmine, is to craft an effective response that reestablishes credibility and takes specific accountability for what I did. For example: "I intended to give you the seat of honor. That didn't happen. Instead, I said something callous and insensitive, and even though I don't deserve it, I hope you'll grant me mercy. Please know that I will never say anything like that to you or anyone else ever again."

Even though it mattered to me, lamenting about how out of character it was for me to say such a phrase would have only have vindicated me and left Jasmine feeling cheated. I needed to objectively assess the damages resulting from my mistake and use that information to focus on solutions that helped everyone move forward. If only I had framed my response around how Jasmine and other people of color would benefit from what I'd learned, I may have had a different outcome and would possibly still be friends with Jasmine today.

So if you ever find yourself in a similar situation, move forward; don't run away. Because the truth about mistakes is you can learn from them. But only if you take what you learned and apply it to future interactions. You have to embrace your missteps, acknowledge the hurt you've caused, and promise to do better—not if, but *when* you're given a second chance.

Learn from Your Mistakes

One such chance occurred for me on a recent April morning, just before Easter. I was shopping at Sephora with my niece, Madison. We approached the checkout lane, laughing and talking about makeup. I dropped my items on the counter and turned my attention back to my niece when I heard a deep voice ask, "Will that be all?"

I said, "Yes sir," just as my eyes shifted over to the clerk, who I then realized was transgender. From the look I received, it was clear the clerk did not want to be called sir, but I didn't know that until after I'd said it. Once I realized my mistake, I smiled intently until the scorn in her eyes vanished. Then I looked at her name tag and said, "Thank you, *Sarah*."

Regardless of your background, beliefs, or political affiliations, the truth is we're all human. And no matter what gender a person identifies with, they still need to know that you care and that they matter.

So how do we do that? We can address people by their names instead of gendered terms like *sir*, *ma'am*, *he*, and *she*. And if we don't know a person's first name, we can stick with gender-neutral phrases, such as *clerk*, *person*, and *friend*. Of course, the clerk was irritated with me when I said, "Yes, sir." It was probably something she's had to deal with all her young life—people flippantly spouting off wrong pronouns and taking zero time to see who she really is.

I know a little bit about that kind of pain because my son, who has long hair and wears brightly colored clothes, is always mistaken for a girl. When he, my daughter, and I go out to eat, servers constantly say, "Hello, ladies." My son also gets funny looks from men and boys when he walks into the men's restroom.

Our world is lightyears away from being gender neutral. Not only do we, as a family, encounter mistaken identity on a regular basis, but my son is also subjected to name-calling and taunts from people who know him.

There's nothing new under the sun. Mean is still mean. When people call him a girl, it infuriates him, and it often devastates me. I can't say what it's like for the clerk I encountered at Sephora, but I imagine it's much worse. That's why, after I made my mistake, I tried to course correct. Hopefully, my smile went a long way in showing her that I cared. Did I mean to show respect when I said, "Yes, sir"? Absolutely. But I did not succeed. From now on, I can reduce my use of pronouns and titles and stop assuming. We can all take the time to find out who people are or give them a chance to tell us themselves.

Make a list of gender-neutral phrases and start using them in everyday conversations. It won't be easy. If you're like me, you've been using gendered words all your life. That's why you have to practice when times are good—so that they roll off your tongue when times are conflicted.

Don't Be Caught Off Guard

The truth about mistakes is they happen when we're caught off guard. For me with Jasmine, alcohol played a part. With Sarah, I was distracted. For you, it could be something as simple as workload. If busyness has ever gotten the best of you, then you know about having to overcome project delays or errors. These purposeful power phrases can help:

- **Be proactive.** "I'll have your plan ready tonight or early tomorrow morning. I just need to tweak the bullets and get a little distance from the content to make sure it's as strong as it can be."

- **Neutralize blame.** "My intent was to get this to you yesterday afternoon. Unfortunately, circumstances outside of my control have resulted in the temporary absence of three of our most critical team members."

- **Show commitment.** "Plans are already underway to reconcile this shortage, and I want to assure you that any errors we've made recently will be made right."

- **Ask for mercy.** "I hope you'll grant us mercy as we work through this. Your patience and understanding are greatly appreciated."

I know my clients have relied heavily on these phrases over the years—Bailey more so than anyone. As a flat-fee retainer client, she learned early on to draw from my services whether her dilemma was business related or personal. Because her schedule was so chaotic, her reputation often depended on both.

The email requests she sent always included the word *help* in all caps with several exclamation points, and I never knew what to expect. One time it was a feud with her in-laws. All members of her husband's family were up in arms trying to schedule Thanksgiving dinner. She graciously agreed to host. However, her sister-in-law Amanda didn't want to make the drive on the date she suggested and was pushing for her to host at an offsite party room under the guise of compromise.

Here's the verbatim HELP!!! email she sent me:

> *"This chick is ridiculous! I'm not moving the location from my house. I'm the only one that offered to host, and most of the people coming live closer to me.*

> *"I basically want to say, 'Screw off! I offered, and it works best at my house.'"*

Here's the reply I wrote for her to send:

> *"Hi Amanda, thanks for surfacing your concerns, and I appreciate your offer to help. It works best for me to host the dinner at my house, but I am totally flexible on the date if you have another preference. Either way, I can always relinquish the hostess role to you if the location is problematic. I'll give you a call this week to discuss. Thanks, Bailey"*

Unfortunately, Bailey sent the entire email chain between her and me to Amanda instead of the power phrase I'd given her. So the "this chick is ridiculous" and "I basically want to say, 'Screw off!'" were included, not to mention evidence that she had used a ghostwriter. We had no choice but to move straight to damage control.

First, because the situation was particularly difficult, I told Baily to use Slydial—a tool I've been using for years to help my CEOs to stay on script when responding to media inquiries. Slydial allows you to connect directly to someone's voice mail without them knowing you've even called. You punch in their cell phone number and get immediately connected to their voice mail. Their phone doesn't ring. This allows you to craft a strong message, stay true to yourself, and deliver a perfect, to-the-point message without getting caught up in a back-and-forth.

Visit truperception.com/thetruthabout to learn more about Slydial

Second, I had to craft a message that helped Amanda believe that Bailey cared about her and that she mattered.

Here's the outline I wrote for the voice mail:

> *"Amanda, I need to ask for your forgiveness. Because I wanted to preserve my relationship with you, I asked my assistant for help in crafting a thoughtful response. However, in explaining the situation, I let my sleep deprivation and work frustrations get the best of me. The things I wrote about you are not true, and I should not have said them. I hope you will forgive me."*

Amanda did eventually forgive Bailey's in-the-moment mistake. Thankfully, the party went off without a hitch, and Bailey and I learned a valuable lesson about slowing down the message-response train.

The truth about mistakes is we can all learn from them. Just remember to stay alert. Don't let them sneak up on you when you're not looking. Otherwise, they'll become moments you'll wish you'd never known.

But what about when mistakes aren't in the moment? What happens when they've been around for so long they feel like the dried-up bones of a corpse?

Chapter 8

The Truth about Skeletons

met Angela at church in 2010, and we became fast friends. Our sons were around the same age, and we spent countless hours at parks, beaches, and every other kid-friendly place. If I had to sum Angela up in two words, they would be *kindergarten teacher*.

She was as soft-spoken, agreeable, and mild mannered as anyone I had ever met. To the outside world, she was the epitome of a doting mom, great friend, and all-around good person. But like many of us, she had a story on the inside that read a bit differently. Four years earlier, Angela had been arrested for felony drug charges and served time in prison.

To understand how Angela went from ex-con to mother of the year, you'd have to know the backstory. And trust me when I say, it's a real heartbreaker. Angela was in her early twenties and attending college when, out of nowhere, her mother was diagnosed with a rare and life-threatening illness. Despite efforts of significant medical and spiritual proportions, her mother died a mere nine days later. Angela's father wasn't in her life, making the void her mother left nearly unbearable. First, her grades slipped until there was nothing left of her academic endeavors. Next, she isolated herself from friends and extended family members. And finally, an unsavory boy entered the picture.

Fast-forward several months later—while driving said boyfriend to a house to pick something up, a swarm of officers arrived on the scene and everyone in sight was arrested. The primary drug culprits eventually got off with a warning on a technicality, but Angela? She was found guilty. Talk about being in the wrong place at the wrong time. To make matters worse (or better, depending on your perspective), Angela learned in prison that she was expecting that boyfriend's baby.

By the time I met Angela, the boyfriend was gone— but that beautiful baby boy was approaching his fifth birthday, and Angela was a college graduate. It was almost the happily-ever-after story of a lifetime, except for one thing: Angela had yet to apply for any jobs.

Why? Because of that pesky little prison skeleton hanging in her closet. She was afraid of the scorn and rejection that she fully believed would come with any interview, so she skirted every opportunity that surfaced. Her anxiety approached record levels, and she began retreating further and further from civilization. Unfortunately, her living situation necessitated an income, and that's when she approached me for help.

The first thing I told her was the truth about skeletons. "Angela, the only person appalled by your prison sentence is you. All you need is a power phrase that doesn't point the finger at the offender (because even a guilty party can assume the underdog role) and preserves your reputation without dwelling on the negative."

She was game, so I set about writing the following message for her to use during interviews and on job applications when requested:

"I've always believed in democracy and abiding by the law. Many years ago, I found myself in a situation where, even though I was innocent, I appeared

*guilty and was charged with a felony drug crime. I
live an honorable life, having served my time, and I
continue to have a strong faith in our justice system.
I have three letters of endorsement here—from the
judge involved in my case, my court liaison, and my
college professor. You'll find their impressions of me
to be extremely favorable."*

What's a court liaison, you ask? That's a probation officer. Call it a power phrase; it means the same thing but
sounds a lot better.

Today, Angela is a gainfully employed, happily married
mom of three children and has no regrets. She offers
encouragement to anyone who's letting a skeleton hold
them back.

I can't tell you how many times people approach me
about skeletons in their closet. It's usually right after
one of my speaking engagements. Their comments typically go like this: "I didn't want to bring my issue up
in front of the group, but . . ." They go on to tell me
about a crime or a poor decision that led to destruction.
Sometimes they're culpable and sometimes they're not.
But what they are all is clueless about how to talk about
their skeleton. They've often never uttered one word of
it in public before.

Unfortunately, the truth about skeletons is that they grow bigger when left in the dark. In any business situation—but especially in a crisis—it's essential not to hide from your employees, clients, and customers. If you do, everyone suffers.

That's why secrets are like gremlins who eat after midnight. The more you do to hide your past or current troubles, the more problematic they become. And before you know it, it's Christmas Eve and a gang of gremlins has destroyed your entire town—or reputation. However, when you shine light on them, gremlins die. It's the same for skeletons; addressing them truthfully can shrink or eliminate them altogether. The key is to be proactive, not defensive, all while quickly assessing risks, considering your audience, and determining the appropriate level of response and how to respond. Sounds easy, right?

It's not, but it can be if you craft the right power phrase. You need to tell the truth, be considerate, and be objective while casting everyone—even yourself—in as favorable a light as possible.

Shine a Light on Your Skeletons

Take bankruptcy. It's a hard truth, and it's happened to many great professionals and business owners. It may seem impossible to divulge this kind of information and not tarnish your reputation, but it can be done. And even if this has never happened to you, learning to craft tough messages will be invaluable if something equally difficult happens in the future.

For one client of mine, the situation was bleak. After twenty years running a family-owned and operated business, Carl got sick. Clients were frustrated when service declined, and the majority started demanding refunds. Within two years the business crumbled under the pressure and declared bankruptcy.

After Carl recovered, the family opened up a new business. Their company was thriving, but they kept encountering difficulties because of their skeleton. They needed a power phrase in their copy bible to showcase their financial stewardship and lessen the negative consequences that occurred when they were too scared to disclose the information or when they fumbled through it. Here's the power phrase I wrote for them:

> *"Eight years ago, a health issue prompted us to make a difficult financial decision, one that we never anticipated having to make—bankruptcy. While I cannot say I'm happy that it happened—it was hard on our employees and their families, and I*

*will always regret that—I can tell you the experi-
ence, while trying, served as a great lesson in how
to manage a business in a worst-case scenario. I'm
thrilled to report that, as a result, we have built
a new business that's not only debt-free but is also
operating with a surplus."*

All the key elements of a power phrase are present here.
The truth is being told. The bankruptcy is revealed. Yet
both the owner and the customers are shown in a favorable light, which is considerate and objective. And this
power phrase does something else too: it bridges to a
positive. The speaker is not left open to rebuttal or additional questions when he pivots to his current debt-free
business status. The listener may even applaud him.

Whenever skeletons are brought out in the open, you
should avoid ending on a negative note. Always move to
the positive, to some current good news or future pos-
sibilities. Don't let your listener decide where you'll go;
take them where you want. Help shift the conversation
away from the skeleton, giving it the least importance
possible.

That's what I did for another client of mine, who hid
her skeleton in a different way. She wasn't avoiding
job opportunities altogether, but she was sidestepping

any person who knew of her skeleton—the reason she stepped down from a highly visible board position.

This was ultimately limiting her ability to make a larger impact on the education industry, which she'd spent her entire life supporting. And it was about to get worse. She was being recognized at a huge charity event where every one of her former associates would be in attendance. After hearing me speak, she approached me for help. Because the institute she'd departed from was floundering, her concern was threefold:

1. She didn't want to be blamed for their shortcomings.

2. She wanted to make it clear she hadn't been asked to step down.

3. She didn't want to dwell on the negative or discredit those involved.

Here's the message I wrote for her:

> *During my tenure with [company], we encountered a challenge—one that had legal and ethical implications. It was difficult, but I carved out a path that would address the issues and restore confidence in our future. Unfortunately, not everyone agreed*

with my plan. When I realized the board was going to go in a direction that no longer aligned with my values, I stepped down.

Nothing is more important to me than continuing my lifelong pursuit of higher education. And that's why I'm leading the [campaign] at [foundation]. We're raising $15 million to rebuild the entire program.

I also gave her a block-and-bridge power phrase to use with cynics who wanted to defame the institute.

"What's important now is that the work continues. And that's why I'm focusing my efforts where I know I can make a difference. Places like [foundation]."

Heal from Your Skeletons

The bad news is that skeletons happen. But just like with crisis, there is good news: About 80 percent of them are common and forgivable. However, you can't wait for someone to take you to task. You must be proactive. Never get caught without some valid talking points. As a leader, remember that you need to develop and practice your worst-case scenario responses now so that you will know what to say when questioned.

Earlier, I said that all Angela needed was a power phrase, but the truth is that she and everyone else with skeletons in their closest need a little more than that. They need to heal. Because the truth about skeletons is they can hurt us.

I know a lot about that. I am someone who has been down in the pit of skeleton misery. For a total of eighteen years, I dated and was married to a methamphetamine addict. The weight of a skeleton of that magnitude doesn't bury you all at once; it happens a little at a time. And, at some point, you can no longer breathe.

The conversations I had with bank tellers about overdraft fees or pawn shop owners trying to retrieve my family heirlooms were the first to take my breath away.

Then it got worse—like the time I pretended I couldn't go on vacation because I didn't want to take money from a savings account that didn't exist. Or having to tell my colleagues that my always absent husband was on a stay-away job. Color my lies white, but they still sucked the air out of my lungs. Yet the stranglehold of my skeleton didn't actually come until after the divorce.

You see, there was no dirtier word in the English language to me than *divorce*. When I say I was opposed to divorce, I mean I was like the NRA opposing anti-gun laws. So not only did I have the skeleton of a broken marriage that screamed of the nastiness of drugs, but I also had a divorce. A word I could not physically speak in reference to myself without gasping for breath.

The Truth Will Set You Free

That was more than a decade ago. Now, the truth about my past rolls off my tongue as easily as a lunch order. But I know, like anyone who's ever had a skeleton, that it didn't come without a cost. The pain was real. And I had to move toward it in order to heal. Some of the first power phrases I ever wrote were for myself. At first, they went something like this: "I didn't get to *stay* married."

That was my only way of telling the truth in a considerate and objective manner without passing out. Over time, I ventured away from the nebulous into a bit of dry humor: "You know the story of *Star Wars*, right? Well, I married Anakin Skywalker. We all know how that turned out. But the good news is I got Luke Skywalker and Princess Leia out of the deal."

Eventually, it didn't hurt to say the word *divorce* or *methamphetamine*, so I got clearer with my descriptions. But I've always saved the harshest elements of the story for my close friends. And there are hundreds of people I've never mentioned it to—but not because I can't. I don't mention it because I no longer see it as being a part of who I am. I knew ultimately that my skeleton was mine and others didn't see it as debilitating as I did. I refused to leave my skeleton in the dark. And even though it hurt me, it didn't kill me.

If you have a skeleton, it won't kill you either. Keep in mind, when you divulge it, some people will affirm you and others may curse you. In the end, it only matters how you view yourself. No one has the right to define you but you and God. Take it from someone who knows firsthand. When I say the truth will set you free, I mean that from the bottom of my heart.

Chapter 9
The Truth about Complaining

"**M**illennials! What's with this generation? They complain about everything. They can't make it to work on time and want nothing to do with the projects they're assigned! They're all just a bunch of trophy kids!"

Every time I hear a baby boomer (or a Gen Xer, like me) utter these words, I chuckle to myself. And then I think, "I wonder what your parents were saying about you in the Sixties or Eighties? I'm sure it wasn't 'Wow, what a great bunch of appropriately satisfied, driven young people.'"

Yet no generation has received more scorn in the workplace than Millennials. They are the poster children for complaining, whining, and refusing to grow up. I'd like to argue a few points about the differences between the three (sometimes four) generations we have in the workforce, and then tell you the truth about complaining. The four generations include:

1. Traditionalists (born before 1950)

2. Baby Boomers (born 1950–65)

3. Gen Xers (born 1965–80)

4. Millennials (born after 1980)

Generational Differences

Most traditionalists have exited the workforce, but some remain. Baby boomers dominate the upper ranks of most companies and are often stereotyped as working long hours and having a never-ending workload. All their lives they've gotten up at six, been in the office by seven, worked through lunch, and left after dark.

On the contrary, Gen Xers are known for ushering in the concept of work-life balance. In other words, coming in and leaving whenever they wanted to. What a lot of people don't realize is *why* Gen Xers did this. And even fewer recognize how they got away with it.

To most baby boomers, Gen Xers seemed lazy. What they actually were was jaded.

Corporate scandals like those of Enron and Arthur Andersen occurred when most Gen Xers were in college or just entering the workforce. Jobs were prevalent, but trust levels were at all-time lows. Gen Xers were the first generation of latchkey kids, coming home to empty houses after school because most had two working parents. Over the years, they watched their Baby Boomer parents working tirelessly and missing out on tons of family time only to be downsized and lose their pensions anyway.

This all caused Gen Xers to think, "That's not going to be me. I'm not going to work every minute of every day for a possibly crooked company that is likely planning to steal my pension." So they started leaving work early to be with their kids.

But here's the thing about Gen Xers: there simply aren't very many of us on the planet. In fact, there are currently thirty million fewer Gen Xers than baby boomers. What that means is when most boomers were up and coming, they had hundreds of people standing in line behind them waiting to take their job if they slacked off. Gen Xers had no one standing in line behind them.

So when they started leaving early to go to their kids' softball games, nothing happened. Their jobs remained intact, and they simply continued pushing the boundaries established by baby boomers until they gained enough personal ground to change the course of workforce history.

Another thing that helped was most Gen Xers knew how to act like boomers. Everywhere they turned, they were inundated with baby boomers, so they learned to speak their language and get the results they wanted. That made turning the tide even easier.

However, the tides are about to turn again. That's because there are just as many millennials in the world as baby boomers. When they all get old enough to enter the workforce, we will see the pendulum swing back to a highly competitive environment where getting exactly what you want might not work anymore.

The thing about millennials is they probably won't care. They'll just start their own businesses. They are highly entrepreneurial and have very little interest in the monetary rewards baby boomers and Gen Xers have always coveted. They want space and freedom to be creative, whether that means going for a run in the middle of the day to generate an idea or watching YouTube clips while writing ads. And they'll get it, even if they have to take a pay cut.

Research shows that millennials care about leadership. And they think having mentors is crucial to their personal success. They also care deeply about making the world a better place and about learning as much as possible.

So the stereotype about millennials is misguided. Of course, there is some truth to it—but that has more to do with youth (and arrogance) than a generation being worse than those before it. The differences between the generations are massive. But trust me when I say, the main similarity is contention. You see, the truth about complaining is everyone does it. Whether you're a baby boomer, Gen Xer, or millennial—entitlement is alive and well.

Every Generation Complains

Several years ago, I was asked by a hundred-year-old, family-owned manufacturing company to help improve morale. More than seven thousand of their employees had responded to a satisfaction survey, and the results were extremely unfavorable. In fact, they were some of the worst I had ever seen.

I went to work on a change engagement that included a cultural audit to inform the CEO of shifts necessary to achieve favorable morale and build a communication plan, centered on a copy bible, so he'd have the right messages to deliver at the right time to get that morale.

During intensive interviews and analyses of their survey data, I surmised that it was baby boomers, not millennials, who were complaining the most. They talked about the "good old days" when profit sharing was plentiful and raises were guaranteed. They protested the idea of pay ceilings and refused to believe that profit margins had anything to do with profit sharing. They wanted what they once had back so badly that they weren't willing to see anything good coming from the company.

Now, in their defense, it was the CEO and his predecessors who had failed to properly communicate socioeconomic changes that necessitated adjustments in pay and benefits over the years. But don't forget the truth about change—those leaders were afraid of looking like bad guys, so they stayed silent.

That doesn't negate the truth about complaining—baby boomers do it just as much as millennials. In fact, ask any leader what the hardest part of their job is, and she or he will probably tell you it's managing the personalities (which are often based on generations) and the interpersonal conflicts of their team.

Unfortunately, the truth about complaining is that leaders don't know how to combat it. That's why leaders—especially new ones—need training. It's not enough to hand them an employee handbook and wish them good luck. Every leader needs to be prepared to navigate the complexities and pitfalls of workplace relationships. I cover this extensively in my management training programs, including the one I built for the hundred-year-old manufacturing company—which was able to improve its morale. Here are just a few of the topics I cover:

Dealing with a Negative Nelly. Emphasize the positive. Try saying, "I need your help. We're behind on the project, and I know that everyone is more productive when morale is up. So let's think of all the good work we're doing and focus on that. I can't do it without you."

Defusing tattletales. Whenever possible, invite the person being tattled on into the conversation. That gets the issues out in the open and facilitates a resolution. It also sets an example for your team on the importance of being transparent and facing conflicts head-on.

Taking sides. Suppose someone you manage complains to you about an increase in the company's healthcare costs. It might feel like the right thing to do is convey sympathy by agreeing. Don't! You have more influence than you realize. You need to be aligned with company goals and values. If you don't trust the company, why should anyone else?

**Visit truperception.com/thetruthabout
to download the guide to managing
workplace relationships**

The truth about complaining is that it is rooted in venting, and even though many people see it as harmless, it's incredibly toxic. It's a nasty habit that's hard to break.

Venting Hurts More than it Helps

I can say with near certainty that we've all found ourselves on the receiving end of the sentence "Can I just vent about so-and-so for a minute?" Engaging in snark talk or spreading rumors are some of the most common faux pas in business diplomacy. And yet no other habit will put your reputation more at risk than complaining. Why? Because despite our seemingly harmless intentions, it can destroy relationships. Not only your relationship with the person you're complaining about but also the relationship with the person you're complaining to.

It doesn't start out that way. In fact, it feels like processing or providing useful information to another person. For example, your conversation might sound something like this: "Roger's a great guy, but he's a bit of a slacker. I mean, the last time he met a deadline, the Beatles had a top-ten record. I'm only telling you this so you can help me save the account. We've worked very hard, and now he may ruin it all. But don't tell Roger I said so. It would only hurt his feelings."

Comments like these place an unfair burden on the recipient, particularly when the information is of a personal nature. And the person you're gossiping with will know that they can't trust you not to talk about them behind their back. Fortunately, there are better communication techniques to use than complaining when negative information needs to be shared:

1. Always assume the person you're talking about will end up hearing whatever you say. That way you'll naturally be more diplomatic. So a comment such as "He's completely incompetent" becomes "I have concerns about his performance."

2. Speak the truth, but do it considerately and objectively. There are always two sides to the story. If you omit your opponents' points of view, you make them the underdogs, and listeners won't align their sympathies with you.

3. Don't say anything that would damage a person's morale or self-worth.

After you've used these techniques to neutralize your comments, here's what to say to ensure confidentiality—and to keep your reputation intact: "Out of respect for Roger, I plan to meet with him to address the issue directly. Therefore, I ask you to hold off on sharing this information with anyone else." You've now made the listener a partner in an honorable process—and a confidante.

Situations will inevitably arise that require talking about people when they're not present. But, whenever possible, preserve everyone's dignity by conducting face-to-face conversations—and cut the gossip out of your life.

But how can you take the moral high road when you're surrounded by complainers? It's not easy, but it is possible. You just need to communicate effectively when confronted by a complainer. Even though it seems people like to vent—especially at someone else's expense—they usually don't. The act of complaining leaves us feeling guilty about saying too much about the wrong thing and rightfully concerned that what we said will come back to haunt us.

Besides, engaging in complaining breeds more complaining, which can easily end up putting your reputation at risk. And if it goes viral on social-media platforms, it can do serious damage to your company's brand. To help you avoid the pitfalls of complaining, here are some scenario-specific phrases that can shut the vicious cycle of negativity down:

Complaining about projects:

- "If that turns out to be the case, then we will take action."

Complaining about people:

- "My preference is to share my opinions about them when they are present."

- "I can't speak for them, but based on the information I have, here's what I can tell you . . ."

Complaining about anything else:

- "Thanks for sharing your insights with me. It's been my experience that . . ."

For maximum effect, follow these phrases by saying something forward-thinking that gets the conversation back on a positive track. You can always start by refocusing the conversation around business strategy. Given the inherent shortcomings of human nature, complaining is hard to avoid. So, when all else fails, walk away. Respect yourself—and others will respect you for it.

When Failure Is the Only Option

Early in my career, I believed—like so many young professionals—that I knew it all. I was overly confident and often guilty of overstating my case. However, when it came to strategic communications, I really did know a lot—even back then. I had not only an inborn ability to influence others but also the education and experience to back it up.

But here's where I always went wrong: Anytime a leader disagreed with one of my brilliant ideas about how to inspire change or promote positive perceptions, I'd fight them to the death, complaining and insisting they fall in line with my thinking or suffer dire consequences. I'd carry on about the drop in productivity or sales that I foresaw. Practically beating my head against the wall, I'd do whatever I could to convince them my way was the right way—the only way.

The trouble was, sometimes they refused to listen and all I did by complaining was drive them further away from my idea. That's why I learned a three-step process for allowing leaders to fail.

- **Explain what's at risk.** Never let someone go down the wrong path without a warning. Say, "Here's what's at risk if you do that," and remind them of the trouble they're likely to encounter if they persist.

- **Let go.** Make it clear that you don't agree with the decision being made and then get out of the way. It's easier to convince them to revisit your plan once they've felt the sting of their wrong choices.

- **Give up the grudge.** Gloating and "I told you so" have no place in a professional arena— but helping a leader find a positive way forward does.

Remember that successful people often say they've learned more from their failures than from their successes. The next time one of your leaders, clients, or vendors wants to make a wrong move—and you can't talk them out of it—let them stumble. Just have your plan in place to help them recover.

Here are some additional communications techniques that can help you communicate better:

- **Know when to change the conversation.** It's healthy to get things off your chest—but not to complain or gripe. All that does is foster negativity. So how do you hear someone out without letting them rant? Simple: the minute they start repeating their main beef, bridge them over to something more positive: "I appreciate you walking me through this, but what we need to focus on now is . . ."

- **Focus on the positive.** Employees who are dissatisfied with their pay and benefits can easily drag their supervisors down into the rabbit hole of "he said, she said." They bring up how much other employees make or how much other companies pay. Instead of trying to answer every single complaint employees raise, change the conversation. Say instead, "There's something that keeps you here on the team. Let's talk about that."

Before You Act...

No matter which decade we were born in, we should all hold ourselves to a higher standard. Complain less, and help others do the same. Be honor bound in your dealings with everyone, whether they're younger, older, or the same age as you, and you'll make the right choices. And now, take a deep breath . . .

. . . because things are about to get a little awkward.

Chapter 10

The Truth about Awkwardness

When I was twenty-one years old, I made a bad decision that led to an incredibly awkward moment, one that I handled with no tact at all. It involved my then ten-year-old sister, Teresa, whom I adored. We were having a blast jetting around town while I was home from college. Throughout the day, we kept stopping back at the house to grab money or drop something off. Each time, I would stop the car in front of our house and let her switch seats with me so that she could pilot the car the last remaining twenty or so feet up into the driveway. I had been allowed to drive when I was ten years old by Teresa's mom, my stepmother. And I thought I was the coolest big sister to ever live.

As the day grew long, Teresa got better and better behind the wheel. So much so that, as we walked out to the car for our last outing of the day, I gave her a sly grin and said, "How would you like to try backing the car out of the drive?"

Right here is where things began to go wrong. Teresa had never driven backward before. In fact, this was likely the first time she'd ever operated any kind of vehicle, let alone an actual car. But that didn't seem to stop me from reaping the cool-sister points she was so eager to give me.

So we jumped into the car, she in the driver's seat and I in the passenger seat. I gave her a few instructions but mainly gushed about how capable and impressive she was at such a tender age. When she seemed ready, I told her to put her foot on the brake and slowly pull the gear shifter into reverse, which she did. But before I could say another word, she slammed her foot on the gas.

We hurtled down the drive so fast my head whipped into the back of the seat and then thrusted forward. All I could see was her foot on the gas, and I started screaming, "Brake, brake, brake!" In milliseconds, we flew across the street, up over the curb and into the neighbor's yard. It was like she couldn't hear me; all she did was bear down harder on the gas.

By some angelic intervention, the car came to an abrupt stop just inches before its back end barreled into the neighbor's front porch. We took one look at each other in sickening despair, saw the neighbors coming out and faster than we'd flown into their yard, jumped out of that car, and ran for our lives.

We sped across their yard and ours. Once inside the house, I screamed commands at my then-husband to get my car and make nice with the neighbors. Because, clearly, I would never be showing my irresponsible, juvenile-driver-enabling face in public again.

And I didn't, at least not in that neighborhood. From that day on, I started parking in the backyard whenever I came home for a visit. Since then, I have learned how to face up to the consequences of my actions, no matter how awkward or mortifying they are.

At its core, the truth about awkwardness is we avoid it at all costs. We run, we hide, and we twist and turn to get away from it.

Dating a Colleague

One area where I see the most difficulties is situations that involve romance. Many people don't know how to talk about dating a colleague. They hide it, which only fuels the office rumor mill and complicates matters. The big problem is secrecy. Keeping quiet about a new (or broken) relationship can significantly compromise both parties' reputations. Rarely is saying nothing the preferred course of action.

The "Me Too" movement further complicates this situation. Some corporate HR departments, including Facebook's and Google's, have drafted office dating policies. Other companies have even prepared "love contracts" for both parties to sign, confirming they weren't coerced into the relationship and that they will act professionally at the office.

Seriously? What we really need is to be better communicators! My advice is simple and can be applied to many challenging situations: to squelch rumors and preserve your reputation, simply be open and honest.

At the beginning of a relationship, take your supervisor aside and say: "I want you to be aware that Jeff and I are considering a more serious relationship. This won't affect our work performance, and we'll use discretion in the office." Do the same for key colleagues. This shows that you're aware of the implications and any repercussions if the relationship fails.

Then stay professional in the office by separating the romance from your duties. Stick to work-related conversations around the office. If the relationship fizzles, be open about it without pointing fingers or holding grudges. And if you find yourself in a particularly sticky situation, like one of my clients who had a speedy divorce and then started dating a colleague, make sure you create some planned power phrases for your copy bible. Such as:

> *"I was in a marriage, and now I'm not. It was hard, but it was good too because I have an amazing daughter."* Pause to allow comments, but regardless of what is said, continue with: *"Here's what I can tell you . . . I'm in a relationship with a coworker. His name is Jeff. We are happy, and everyone is well."*

Then be prepared to block and bridge with the following immediate power phrases:

- "Jeff will need to speak to that. Here's what I can tell you . . ."

- "I wouldn't say that."

- "Not exactly; let me explain . . ."

If accused of anything specific, say,

> *"My intention is to always promote a professional working relationship with Jeff. Because we are in a relationship, I understand your interest. However, my preference is to talk about this when he's present and for us to focus on [project]."*

Responding to Invasive Questions

The truth about awkwardness is we think we have to answer every question asked of us, even if they're inappropriate. We don't. All we need are immediate power phrases in our pocket that tell the truth and are considerate and objective. Don't let people drag you anywhere you don't want to go. Take the following thinly veiled insults camouflaged as innocent questions. Each response option affords you control over the conversation in a diplomatic manner:

"You're pretty young to be working here, don't you think?"

- "Thank you for the compliment."

- "My accomplishments speak for themselves."

- "I hope to feel this young forever."

"How old are you?"

- "I'm as old as I need to be to . . ."

"How come you're still single?"

- "I'm exactly where I want to be. I have friends and a solid career, and I'm healthy."

- "I'm open to interacting with anyone who will add value to my life."

- "I want to answer most of your questions. Do you have another one?"

"How much do you weigh?"

- "I weigh the exact amount necessary to be as strong as I am."

Responding to Innocuous Questions

Likewise, sometimes someone asks a seemingly innocent question, but the answer is long and difficult. For example, "Where are you from?" is innocent enough, but when the answer is complicated because you don't know your heritage or you grew up in foster care, it can be hard to know what to say. Similar questions can be asked about marriage, family, adopted children, and stepchildren.

The idea here is to always have a power phrase in your copy bible ready to deliver to inquisitive others. Tell them only what you're comfortable sharing and be prepared to block and bridge if they probe (innocently or invasively) for more. Such as:

- "I've lived all over, but I now call Minnesota home."

- "We are a family of three. It's me and my two sons."

- "I know enough about my heritage to say that I am from Asia."

- "I've had three committed relationships in my life and each one blessed me with a child."

Here are a few innocuous but still awkward situations that the average person encounters and some ways to address them:

- **You need to ask a new boss for time off.** Say, "Hi, Gary, I'm very excited to start with the new team on May 1. Thanks again for the opportunity. Because I have a previously scheduled vacation starting on May 23, I want to let you know right away in case there are any scheduling conflicts we need to work around. I will be traveling to Asia for twelve days. Please let me if you have any questions or concerns. Thanks."

- **You're invited to a lunch or dinner and you really don't want to go.** Say, "Because my workload is so intense right now, I'm holding myself to a strict work schedule. However, I would like to connect. Let's look at our calendars and see if there are any networking events we're both attending. Perhaps we can sit together then."

- **Responding to a perceived romantic invitation from someone you're not interested in.** Say, "I'm open to a platonic friendship if that's what you have in mind," or, "You hold on to your number, and I'll hold on to mine. It was great meeting you."

- **If you're asked to "help out" a friend:** Especially if the ask is work related, propose two kinds of assistance by asking, "Is this a favor or billable?"

Derailing Offensive Comments

Most people mean well. It just doesn't occur to them that they're being offensive. However, some have ill intentions. For times when straight-up insults shoot your way, these power phrases should do the trick:

Your boss calls you a slacker: Never laugh that off. Say, "I'm going to need you to clarify that comment. In what way am I not meeting expectations?"

A coworker takes credit for your work: Don't stoop to their level; instead stay focused on the positive. Say, "I want to clear up a potential misunderstanding about how my contributions to this project are being conveyed."

A client tries to put words in your mouth: Never let others speak for you. If a client says, "So you pretty much hate working for that guy," respond with "I wouldn't say that. Here's what I can tell you . . ."

Friendships at work are always tricky. One of my CEO clients, Rebecca, hired a fractional CFO to get her company's financial house in order. Within the first week, her leadership team reported that the CFO was questioning Rebecca's business model and critiquing her decisions. In part, the CFO was speaking her mind, but she was also trying to make friends with members of the team and had little else to talk about. To help Rebecca keep productivity levels high and morale in check, I wrote the following power phrase for her to use with the CFO:

> *"For the time being, please hold off on sharing any thoughts you have about me, my leadership style, or the decisions I'm making now or in the past until I'm there with you. That way I can offer my perspective and my team will see that you and I are aligned. In the meantime, please continue getting to know the team. Many employees will share information about family and hobbies."*

Here are a few more practical power phrases to help you regain control when an awkward situation threatens to derail your reputation or call it into question:

An employee starts screaming about a vendor. Temper their outburst with a comment such as, "Help me understand how I can help you deal with this issue."

Inappropriate comments or jokes are made Say, "I understand that you mean well and wish to lighten the mood. However, I need you to speak favorably about other cultures." If someone is talking unkindly about anyone or addressing topics or using language that isn't appropriate for those around them, a simple, "Be appropriate," will suffice in a pinch. However, feel free to include, "My preference is for us to speak favorably about . . ."

Letting a vendor go. Get them on the phone right away and say, "We've decided not to move forward, and here's why." You don't have to divulge every detail behind your decision, but they'll feel better if they get at least one reason. They'll probably counter, but simply stick to your message and politely end the conversation.

When Awkward is Helpful

The truth about awkwardness is sometimes it changes us for the better. When I was eighteen, I worked as a trainer for a small-town telemarketing company where two leaders blessed me with the rudest, most poorly delivered advice I've ever received.

It happened with the first leader the moment we met. After shaking my hand, he looked me straight in the eye and said, "Your hand feels like a slimy, dead fish." The second leader accosted me for complaining about being heckled by a colleague in front of a room full of trainees. Rather than vindicate me, she said, "It sounds like you're a baby who doesn't know how to take charge."

While painful to hear, both pieces of advice changed my life for the better: I immediately firmed up my handshake and mastered conflict negotiations. Today, my philosophy on giving and receiving advice is grounded in those experiences, with the following caveats:

- **Don't be shy.** It can be awkward, especially with a stranger, but some advice is worth the risk. You'd want to know if your fly was down or you had food in your teeth, right? Once the embarrassment subsides, you may even be rewarded with a thank-you.

- **Use tact.** Insults may spur attentiveness, but always be considerate. If a coworker is using all caps in an email, say, "Readers see all-cap messages as an angry shout. Consider using colored or bold text instead."

- **Keep it up.** Even if a recipient's initial response is negative, that doesn't mean he or she won't see its benefit to them later on. Show positive intent, and remember that you could be the catalyst for a life-changing event.

We think there's a magical way to get results without being direct. There isn't. Honesty really is the best policy. Here are the precise words to manage a *helpful* scenario without damaging your reputation.

If someone has bad breath or heavily scented perfume, you can say to them: "Professional appearance is an important part of this job. I understand you may feel comfortable with your appearance, and I wish I were approaching you about a different topic. However, I need us to talk about [our dress code, your hygiene efforts]."

This template works well if the individual you're approaching suffers from halitosis, but it also works for when someone brings food with strong odors into the office, making others nauseous. People who chew their food loudly or exhibit any other poor table manners can be addressed with this template as well.

In fact, any type of unknown tendency, even someone who stares longingly at one or many people in the office, can be addressed using this template. All you have to do is swap out the details of the first awkward situation with the next one. That's because it tells the truth in a considerate and objective way and casts everyone in as favorable a light as possible.

For example:

> *"Employees need to feel safe and secure at all times. I understand you may feel comfortable with how you interact with your coworkers, and I wish I were approaching you about a different topic. However, I need us to talk about your tendency to look intently at women in the office.*

> *"What ideas do you have for how you can adjust your eye contact so that everyone feels comfortable? I'm happy to share my ideas as well."*

Norm of Reciprocity and Oversharing

In my youth, while visiting colleges down south, I learned a lesson about myself and others that remains with me to this day. It happened at a small church service near the campus of one school I'd visited. After the service, I was standing near the door, saying hello to people, when a woman approached me. I said, "Hello. How are you?" She then proceeded to tell me the most intimate details of a recent hysterectomy she'd undergone, asking me to hold her baby while she pointed out some of the more visible scars.

Most people tend to be matchers and follow the norm of reciprocity, disclosing at a similar level. Not this woman.

She ignored the rules and went straight to revealing information about herself that I had not invited. And she wasn't the last. All my life, everywhere I go, people overshare.

I consider it a blessing. Not only is it fodder for my blogs and books, but it also allows me to help more people. However, the average person isn't as likely in favor of having someone overshare. So how do you respond in social or business settings where the expectation is polite discourse and you get oversharing about any of the following?

- Their ex or soon-to-be ex

- Their new diet that you should try

- Their detailed medical history

- All the reasons they dislike their boss/job/ coworkers

Simple: Always give your colleague a short, specific window of time to share. Rather than using generic phrases like "I have a few minutes" or "a little bit of time," say, "Because I have six minutes before my next meeting, let's focus on how I can help you."

This forces everyone, consciously or not, to truncate their topic because they know the clock's ticking.

When Awkwardness Can't Be Avoided

The truth about awkwardness is sometimes it can't be avoided. Life is hard, and tragedies occur. When they do, a deeper level of awkwardness exists, and that predicates a deeper level of consideration. Whether you know a colleague who's going through a divorce, just lost their pet, or was diagnosed with cancer, avoid closed-ended, yes-no questions like, "Are you okay?" They never fare well when you're trying to instill a sense of care and concern. Instead, ask open-ended questions, like, "What do you need the most right now from me?" Let them share as they see fit. In times like these, people need a listening ear, so keep your comments brief and your prompts frequent.

If you innocently ask, "How's work?" and your friend says, "Oh, I got fired," ask an open-ended question or comment to encourage more favorable dialogue. Say, "Tell me about your future plans." To easily avoid the tripping over your tongue, replace a narrow question like, "How's work?" with open-ended phrases or questions like, "Tell me about you," or "What's the update on you?" That way you won't accidentally broach a sensitive subject.

With one of the deepest issues you can encounter, a suicide of a spouse or child of someone you know, the most important thing is to use the deceased's name. People often omit it in the case of suicide because they're shocked and they don't know what to say. This inadvertently makes it worse on survivors.

"I was shocked and saddened to hear about Jillian. There truly aren't words to describe the sadness I feel for you and your entire family. I will be thinking of you and wishing you comfort as you remember every wonderful moment you had with Jillian."

Before You Act...

Remember, at its core, the truth about awkwardness is we avoid it at all costs. And when we do attempt to address it, we often stumble through our approach. But awkwardness can change us for the better. So, when someone offers you advice—whether it's good or bad, warranted or not—give it serious thought. Who knows? Someday you may want to thank them. Most importantly, whenever awkwardness can't be avoided, extend as much care and concern to your colleagues as possible.

If you're on the receiving end of such consideration, you'll definitely appreciate it, especially if you already know the perils of harassment.

Chapter 11
The Truth about Harassment

With the onslaught of media about sexual harassment and abuse, it's important that women and girls have the copy bible language they need to stay in control during uncomfortable situations. Too many women haven't had the benefit of this kind of coaching, and unfortunately an untrained response may intensify the situation, adding fuel to the fire. Most importantly, everyone needs to know they don't have to engage in a conversation that makes them uncomfortable. There's a better way.

Take, for example, a local male colleague of mine. It's common knowledge that he stands a little too close, demands hugs, and wants to pull women onto his lap. At business and social events that he frequents, I've seen many women concede. It could be that they like him and have no problem with his advances. Or perhaps they feel compelled to comply even though they don't want to.

If the latter is true, that's a problem for me. And I always ask if they want my advice.

I tell those that say yes to, first, clearly and considerately state their boundaries. Say, "My preference is for you to stand a little further back. If I'm ready for a hug, I'll let you know." We don't need to make excuses for wanting our own personal space. And we don't need to let anyone into that space without our consent.

Second, rinse and repeat. Don't let him mistake your intentions as humorous. If he acts like you're kidding, tell him again just as confidently. Repeat kindly until he gets it. Finally, if he won't take nice for an answer, be firmer and then leave.

Unfortunately, though, the truth about harassment is sometimes you can't leave. Sometimes it's your boss. Sometimes, it's your livelihood.

When You're Not Sure It's Harassment

Several years ago, a client of mine, Susie, told me about a dinner she attended with a new male boss. It was at a hotel restaurant during a business trip. As soon as she sat down, her boss asked, "So do you like to party?"

Susie was absolutely floored and didn't know how to respond, but eventually stuttered out, "I mean, I enjoy an occasional glass of wine, but I wouldn't say I like to party." Her response is much too common when dealing with conflict. Because we want to make positive impressions, we steer clear of rocking the boat and, unfortunately, get dragged down into a potential rabbit hole of harassment.

Susie didn't want to answer that question—but she felt like she had no choice. Whenever it seems like their personal brand is at stake, many people will say almost anything to keep it intact. Susie didn't want to come across as a prude or a spoilsport, but she didn't want to open herself up to innuendo either. So she took the safe route: teetering somewhere between party animal and church girl.

But she didn't have to do any of that. I told her a different response to his awkward question would have allowed her to regain control of the conversation and steer it to a more comfortable topic. My suggested response: "I haven't given that much thought. What I have given thought to is tomorrow's presentation. And I have a couple questions for you." If a conversation makes you uncomfortable, disengage from it. You are not obligated to answer every question that is asked of you.

Of course, these words are not the silver bullet to the pervasive problem of sexual harassment. My goal here is to help women and men more confidently manage those situations when someone crosses the line of what's socially acceptable. Words alone may not stop an aggressive attack. It isn't that easy. But I do hope they make everyone feel more powerful during awkward advances.

Hugs don't always have sexual overtones. And the question "Do you like to party?" may have simply been a well-meaning invitation to a company-sponsored evening event. But if you find yourself in an uncomfortable position, here are some other communication techniques that may put a halt to harassment before it begins:

- **Stick to business topics.** Demonstrate through your demeanor and word choice what is and is not appropriate for conversation. If you catch yourself straying, simply course correct with a phrase like, "Let's get back to the agenda."

- **Stand your ground.** If your assailant persists, ask them to stop. A simple statement such as "Be appropriate" usually suffices. But when in doubt, be more direct.

- **Don't overreact.** Unless you feel threatened, keep your emotions in check. People often test the waters to see how far you'll let them take a certain topic. Once you establish clear boundaries, they're likely to adhere to them.

- **Get help when necessary.** Document instances of inappropriate behavior and share that information with an HR representative. However, be careful not to discuss the offending situation with more than one or two confidants. Doing so could lead to your being perceived as just another office gossip.

When You're Sure It's Harassment

However, if you find yourself in the middle of a harassment issue like one of my clients, let me show you how to create boundaries on appropriate work-related behavior. Because the truth about harassment is you need support.

When Alicia approached me for help, I asked her to tell me what happened. Here's what she said:

> *"A few months ago, a customer came up behind me at my desk and rubbed my shoulders and kissed my head while I had a different customer at my desk. I was horrified. I told my manager, and he said he would talk to the customer. The customer still comes into the store and often says inappropriate comments to one of the clerks. Oftentimes when he walks in, he and my manager sit in his office chatting and laughing. Other times when he comes in, my boss will go hide and tell me to let him know when he's gone because he doesn't have time for him."*

Alicia then asked, "Do I call HR, tell my boss how I feel, or find a new job?"

I said, "Because your employer has a responsibility to ensure an environment that is free of unwanted touch, even with regard to customer interaction, you should go to HR if your manager is not responding." I went on to say that prior to approaching HR, she should talk with her manager using the following language:

> *"I need your help. I remain uncomfortable with Jerry because of the incident that occurred on May*

19, which I shared with you that day. I understand you rely on me to help with customers. However, my preference with Jerry is for you to be the one having direct communications with him. I'm also looking to you for a plan on how to resolve the issue with Jerry. How would you like for us to proceed with that?"

I then gave Alicia instructions on how to respond to the following reactions from her boss:

- **If he disagrees:** Let him know that you're setting up a meeting with HR to get help.

- **If he says he doesn't know what to do:** Tell him that HR will know what to do and that he should set up a meeting with them.

- **If he needs to think about it:** Ask for the date when he will be ready to proceed with a plan.

Whether Alicia gets the results she's seeking has a lot to do with how well her boss supports her. But even if he won't support her, HR likely will. If you find yourself in a similar situation, here's what you need to do when approaching HR:

Document the situation, including:

- Dates and times of the incidents with precise facts of what occurred

- Dates and times that you've expressed
  concern to your manager

- Any response your manager has provided or
  issue resolution plans that have been made

In general, be mindful of the use of emotionally charged words like "assault." Even if that's what it felt like, it's important to stick to the facts in the documentation.

If neither your boss nor HR offer you support, then it's time to evaluate a potential job move. Your physical and emotional well-being may depend on it. Because the truth about harassment is it rarely goes away on its own.

While sexual harassment is the most common form of harassment in the workplace, hostile environment and retaliation occur as well.

When Your Workplace Is Hostile

A good friend of mine is a college professor. She is currently in an environment in which her dean consistently makes discriminatory comments that interfere with her work and create an offensive environment. I witnessed this firsthand when I served as a panelist for one of her classes. The dean asked challenging questions, talked over my friend, and called her credibility into question. His demeanor was so volatile that I thought he was a disgruntled nontraditional student. When I learned he was the dean of the university, I was shocked. He seemed as far from a faculty member as a person could be, let alone a man who held a high-ranking position.

Aside from what I saw, the dean has made jeering comments about my friend's ethnic background, attire, and interests. He's usurped her authority in meetings and mocked her to individual students. In fact, she has a folder hundreds of pages deep documenting each incident.

Unfortunately, for the dean's actions to be considered harassment, my friend needs to prove that they're based on her race and gender. They likely are, but proving that is often difficult. To make matters worse, when she first reported the situation to her boss, the dean was informed and the very next day her car was vandalized. If the dean is found to have been involved, he could face retaliation charges as well.

My friend currently has a pending lawsuit. The power phrases she has to use with herself, her colleagues, and the dean each day to manage the turmoil and teach her classes are virtually endless. I honestly haven't heard her laugh in months.

Harassment is no laughing matter. Unfortunately, I cannot tell you how many times it's treated as such. Everyone enjoys a good joke, unless, of course, they happen to be the butt of it. Then it's not nearly as much fun.

Let's face it: words can hurt, especially in the workplace where professional courtesies ought to be the norm. But there are steps you can take to minimize the pain. For starters, know what to say to neutralize even the most trying situations, and anytime your opponent excuses their behavior by saying, "I was just kidding," don't let them off the hook so easily.

Suppose someone always refers to you as "Blondie" and you don't like it. The next time it happens, respond with a neutralizing yet actionable statement such as "I'd prefer it if you'd address me by my first name." If they reply by saying, "Oh gosh, I was just kidding," hold your ground: "That may be so. But my preference is still for you to refer to me by my name."

A word of caution: In defending yourself against an offensive jokester, check with friends or colleagues to make sure you're reading the situation correctly. Do other people see this person as harmless? Then perhaps you're being oversensitive.

Before You Act...

In all personal interactions, the one thing you *can* control is your feelings. So, if a leopard won't change his or her spots, don't devolve into a scold. Instead, focus on not letting the offending party get to you. After all, words can only hurt us if we let them.

I realize that's tough to do in the moment, especially if your harasser is your boss. If necessary, get the support you need from HR or a lawyer. Harassment is not something to stay silent about. You need words that make you feel able, not uncomfortable. And those words always spill the truth while being considerate and objective.

Conclusion

Fear threatens to paralyze even the best leaders. But you're never at the mercy of your circumstances; you can come from a position of power and influence others, even in the most difficult situations.

Just don't try to wing it. Get your communication house in order and never be caught off guard. Create immediate and planned power phrases and house them in your copy bible.

Remember, people want to know that you care about them as individuals and that their work matters. If every message you convey includes an element of truth, consideration, and objectivity, you will succeed in combating any crisis, sabotage, or change you encounter. And you'll know exactly how to shut down the haters in your life who are out to get you.

Having been a skeleton-holder and someone who has made mistakes, I know how hard all of this is. Sometimes two degrees and more than two decades of experience in the field of communication help me, and sometimes they do not. We are all human, and perfection will never be ours. Yet we can hold ourselves to a higher standard.

Speeches, Coaching, Workshops, and Ghostwriting

My vision is to reestablish a communications ethic that inspires millions of people to speak and write the truth considerately and objectively. Will you join me? If so, I'd like to hear from you.

My corporate years presented me with countless opportunities to craft strategic messages that helped to drive change, manage crises, boost engagement, and build brand awareness. The best practices gleaned from this experience are the lifeblood of the services and tools I offer—services I hope you'll take advantage of to gain the skills and confidence you need for success.

To get on my calendar, call 763-670-6701 or email me at melissa@truperception.com.